Put a Fan
in Your Hat!

Also by Robert S. Carrow
Turn on the Lights–From Bed!

Put a Fan in Your Hat!

Inventions, Contraptions, and Gadgets Kids Can Build

Robert S. Carrow

Illustrations by Rick Brown

LEARNING
TRIANGLE
PRESS

Connecting
kids, parents, and teachers
through learning

An imprint of McGraw-Hill

New York San Francisco Washington, D.C. Auckland Bogotá Caracas
Lisbon London Madrid Mexico City Milan Montreal New Delhi
San Juan Singapore Sydney Tokyo Toronto

McGraw-Hill

A Division of The **McGraw·Hill** *Companies*

©1997 by **The McGraw-Hill Companies, Inc.**
Published by Learning Triangle Press, an imprint of McGraw-Hill.

pbk   1 2 3 4 5 6 7 8 9 DOC/DOC 9 0 2 1 0 9 8 7 6
hc   1 2 3 4 5 6 7 8 9 DOC/DOC 9 0 2 1 0 9 8 7 6

Product or brand names used in this book may be trade names or trademarks. Where we believe that there may be proprietary claims to such trade names or trademarks, the name has been used with an initial capital or it has been capitalized in the style used by the name claimant. Regardless of the capitalization used, all such names have been used in an editorial manner without any intent to convey endorsement of or other affiliation with the name claimant. Neither the author nor the publisher intends to express any judgment as to the validity or legal status of any such proprietary claims.

Library of Congress Cataloging-in-Publication Data
Carrow, Robert S.
    Put a fan in your hat! : inventions, contraptions, and gadgets kids can build / Robert S. Carrow ; illustrations by Rick Brown.
        p. cm.
    Includes index.
    Summary: Encourages and fosters the spirit of invention by describing how to build such gadgets as a homemade motor, a hat with a fan in it, and a motorized shoe buffer.
    ISBN 0-07-011657-1. — ISBN 0-07-011658-x (pbk.)
    1. Inventions—Juvenile literature. 2. Children as inventors—Juvenile literature. [1. Inventions.]
I. Brown, Rick, ill. II. Title.
T339.C349 1996
608—dc20
                                                            96-41247
                                                                CIP
                                                                 AC

McGraw-Hill books are available at special quantity discounts to use as premiums and sales promotions, or for use in corporate training programs. For more information, please write to the Director of Special Sales, McGraw-Hill, 11 West 19th Street, New York, NY 10011. Or contact your local bookstore.

Acquisitions editor: Judith Terrill-Breuer
Editorial team: Executive editor: Lori Flaherty
                Managing editor: Andrew Yoder
                Book editor: April Nolan
                Indexer: Jodi L. Tyler
Production team: DTP supervisor: Pat Caruso
                DTP operators: Kim Sheran, Tanya Howden
                DTP computer artist supervisor: Tess Raynor
                DTP computer artists: Nora Ananos, Charles Burkhour, Steve Gellert, Charles Nappa
Designer: Jaclyn J. Boone
                                                                              SIES3

To my son, Ian Matthew Carrow,
who helped out with the projects (some were even his ideas).
May he and all children always continue to create,
invent, and contribute. We need this from them!

Contents

Introduction
So you want to invent...

Yes, I said stop! Don't skip ahead to the projects yet! This book can give you hours of fun and some really cool projects, but you're going to need a little help before you begin. So here it is.

Profile of an inventor

If the shoe fits, wear it. In other words, if you think you could be an inventor, be one! All types of people can invent. There are educated inventors, absent-minded inventors, and lucky inventors (people who were in the right place at the right time). Those lucky inventors were not only in the right place at the right time—they also had the smarts to recognize an opportunity because they had their eyes and ears open. They were constantly on the lookout for ideas, components for their ideas, and opportunities to use their ideas. The inventor of the future (you?) has to be ready!

Put a Fan in Your Hat!

The following list describes qualities common to inventors. If you have at least five of these qualities, you're on your way to being an inventor yourself! How many do you have?

1 Inventors are resourceful
When inventors need a part or component, they find it. They believe it can be found or it can be done!

2 Inventors are always thinking, and thinking ahead
Whenever inventors have time to kill, they are thinking constructively by asking themselves questions about the world around them.

3 Inventors are pack rats
They collect anything and everything, knowing that someday, for some project, they might need that special something as part of an invention.

4 Inventors take learning seriously   An education can only help the young inventor know more. Knowing more can lead to more ideas!

5 Inventors ask a lot of questions   If they don't know why something works, they ask. Then they know!

6 Inventors are adventurous Whenever someone is going to throw away an old appliance or device, inventors get it and take it apart. They might find a part they need or actually see how something works, but they know this can help them invent.

7 Inventors read and write Famous inventors have to be able to read and write well. (They won't become famous if they can't document their work.) Reading can give you the basic understanding of practically everything. Whether you read books, magazines, or the newspaper, you are learning and getting ideas.

8 Inventors doodle
Another related skill inventors
should have is the ability to
sketch. If an inventor draws
a picture of an invention
ahead of time, he or she
can work out problems on
paper before wasting time
and money on the actual
project. But sketching is
also good for those who
are being shown what the
invention can do.

9 Inventors are patient   If inventors weren't patient, they
would go crazy when things didn't work. The saying, "If at
first you don't succeed, try, try again," applies here.

10 Inventors "mind exercise"   Ask lots of questions. Wonder
about everything! A healthy mind is a creative one.

Of course, there are no guarantees in life when it comes to
success. But if you never try, you'll never succeed, either.
Inventors are like explorers: They try new things, think of creative
ways to solve problems, and basically have fun. You can be this
person . . . and if you're reading this book, you *are* this person!

Whatever your reason to invent, always strive to make it fun and
rewarding. Never invent under pressure. Give yourself plenty of
time because you can absolutely count on running into surprises
and obstacles along the way, and these will take time and
thought to overcome.

Reading books about famous inventors can be helpful, too. Books about Benjamin Banneker, Marie Curie, Thomas Edison, Nikola Tesla, and other inventors and scientific pioneers will tell you about other young inventors and the way they lived. Get involved with science clubs. Visit your local science museum. Participate in science fairs and contests whenever you can. Don't worry about winning; just go to the fairs and observe who wins and with what projects.

The inventor's challenge

You, as an inventor, have accepted a challenge: to solve a particular problem. Have you ever heard the saying, *necessity is the mother of invention*? It's a fancy way of saying that if you need something, you'll find a way to get it. Engineers, scientists, and inventors all create because they *need* something for some purpose.

Inventing—and, really, science in general—is about taking this need or problem and asking questions about *how* to solve it until you come up with a *way* to solve it. Sometimes a solution is not ideal because it's too expensive or it takes too long or it isn't practical. In that case, you need to keep asking questions until you come up with something that will solve the problem perfectly for you.

Put a Fan in Your Hat!

Inventor M.O.
(Modus Operandi, method of operation)

Once you have accepted the challenge to solve a problem, you need to develop a plan of attack. Start with paper and pencil (with an eraser, so that you can erase when you need to change something). Write at the top of the page the problem and the proposed solution. The solution is your goal. Next, list all the steps you could take to reach your goal. This list should include materials, procedures, and a sequence. Remember that you have to do the first things first!

Let's use the fan in the hat on the cover of the book as an example of this kind of scientific thought. You'll need to have a question-and-answer session with yourself, like this:

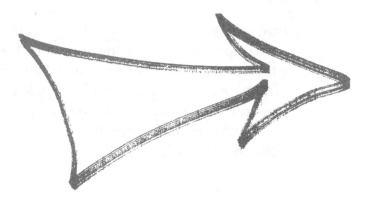

What's the problem?

I need to shade my eyes from the sun on a hot day, but wearing a hat makes me even hotter.

What's the solution?

I could make a hat that will keep my head cool instead of hot.

How do I do that?

Well, I could put an air conditioner under my hat.

What's wrong with that solution?

It would probably be a little uncomfortable carrying 60 pounds or more of metal on my head. (And where would I plug myself in?

I definitely need to ask some more questions.)

What's a better way to tackle the problem?

Put something on my hat that is much smaller, and battery-operated, but will still keep me cool on a hot day.

⭐ In other words, put a fan in my hat!

Put a Fan in Your Hat!

While you are putting your list together, draw or sketch your idea or invention in pencil on a separate piece of paper. This will help you think of the logic and the steps you need to take to build it. Then try to draw it *to scale*, with all the associated parts proportional in size to each other. A good sketch should have plenty of erase marks—so should the project-planning sheet. The more erase marks, the better, because this shows that you're thinking! Putting a working concept on paper is how inventions start.

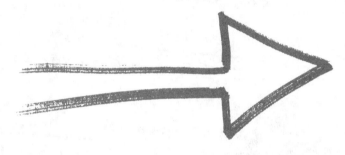

You, as a young inventor, have the luxury of getting second opinions from people like your parents. Bounce your idea off them to see what they think. If they like it, your next move may be to ask them to finance your project. (Of course, if you bring them on as investors, you have to share the rewards later. That's the rule!)

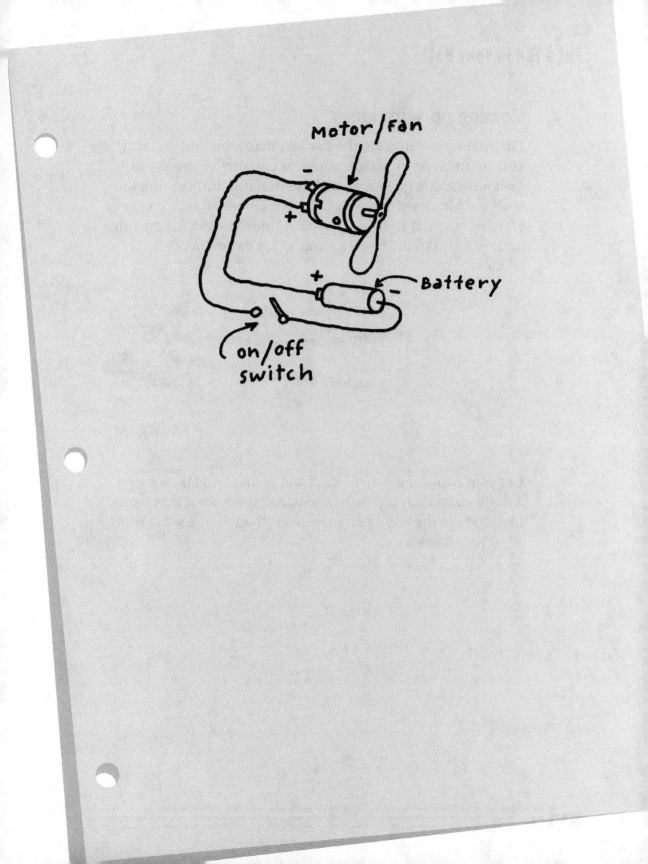

Motor/fan

Battery

on/off
switch

Coming up with ideas

Original ideas often are the hardest items to come by. Maybe
you are the type of person who can complete a project or
assignment quickly once you have the idea, but coming up
with the idea itself takes forever. Remember *pressure creativity*
(forcing yourself to invent) usually doesn't work for anyone,
adults or children. Here's a simple way to get plenty
of ideas.

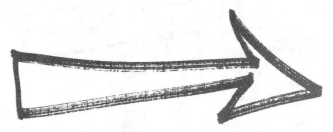

Get your paper and pencil again and go out and take a survey.
Ask 10 adults their top three needs. Ask them what they would
like to see in the way of an invention. Then do the same with
10 of your friends.

Friends

1 Name

2 Name

3 Name

4

5

6

7

8

9

10

a. Need or invention # 1
b. Need or invention # 2
c. Need or invention # 3

a.
b.
c.

a.
b.
c.

Put a Fan in Your Hat!

Hint: If you can be specific in your questions and ask them in a simple-answer format, you might get better results. For example, instead of asking, "What would you invent to help the world?" you might ask two or three related questions to get your answer.

1 Old automobile tires are bad for the environment, right?

2 What practical uses can you think of for old tires?

3 Can you think of any better uses for old tires?

Let your parents and friends create for you! After the actual survey, tabulate your answers. If there is a similar frequent answer, there is a possibility that the majority of the population wants it! Regardless, you have just gotten yourself sixty or so ideas.

Yes/No Survey Form (sample)

Question #1
old Automobile tires are bad for the environment, right?

Name	Yes	No
1 Bill Smith	X	
2 John Jones	X	
3		
4		
5		
6		
7		
8		
9		
10		
Totals		

Question #2
What pratical uses are there for old tires?

Name	Answers

Young inventors become old inventors

Using your inquisitive nature at an early age will make you inquisitive as an adult, too. You may go into engineering, medicine, repair or service of products, or leading-edge technologies (computers, electronics, etc.). Or you may be an artist, a writer, an architect. And remember: Doctors have invented machines and devices to help people, and attorneys have invented safer playground toys. Remember if there's a need and you can fill it, you are inventing!

So starting asking yourself these questions about everything you encounter:

☞ **What's the problem?**

✻ **How can I solve it?**

✳ **What do I need?**

✳ **How do I do it?**

✰ **When can I get started?**

The answers to those questions are up to you to find...except for that last one. You can get started right now!

How to use this book

Put a Fan in Your Hat! focuses on making useful and fun projects that solve problems and that really work. Your project or invention won't be available in any store, so you'll have the only one like it in the world—especially if you customize it with unique parts that only you might have!

But more importantly, this book teaches you how to think like an inventor. Once you can do that, you can invent all kinds of gadgets to make your life easier and more fun. And with a little inspiration, you might be able to make someone else's life easier one day. Who knows? Maybe the invention you make will be the next hot product marketed throughout the world.

> **The cookie problem** Each project in the book will provide you with a chance to "fill a need" in two different ways. The first version calls for off-the-shelf (or ready-to-use) components. You can assemble these parts fairly quickly, but store-bought components are a little expensive. The second version will require you to search for materials and parts you can put together or adapt to fit the project.

Put a Fan in Your Hat!

This will take more time, but it will cost a lot less. Both versions of the same project will be fun to build and fully operational, and, of course, they will solve the problem you need to solve. But because this book is really about going further and coming up with your own solutions, the second version is a little more challenging.

A good way to think of two solutions to one problem is to think of a nice, gooey, chocolate-chip cookie. Mmmm, can't you taste it now?

Well, since you're thinking like a scientist, how are you going to solve this problem of wanting a homemade chocolate-chip cookie?

The just-add-water solution One solution is to buy a box of cookie mix, add water, and bake cookies. You get your cookies pretty quickly, but you have to spend more money; you might not realize it, but cookie mix costs a lot more per serving than the individual ingredients cost. And making cookies this way doesn't let you adjust the recipe and add other ingredients, like nuts or marshmallows.

The make-it-from-scratch solution Another solution to the cookie problem is to gather up butter, sugar, and vanilla and mix them together. Add eggs. Then add some milk. Slowly add some flour. Mix again. Then add some chocolate chips and mix again. And then bake the cookies. With this solution, you have to scrounge around for the stuff you need and put it all together in the right order. It takes longer, but because you're making it yourself, from scratch, you can use your imagination and create the perfect cookie for you. You can be inventive!

Whether you're baking cookies or building an automatic fish feeder, there are always several ways to tackle the problem.

What's important is asking questions and trying to answer them. The best answers aren't even in this book, because you haven't asked them yet!

So read on, future Marie Curie, Christine Mann Darden, Thomas Edison, Albert Einstein, John Slaughter, or George Westinghouse. Those people are all famous scientists who started out as ordinary people who asked questions, thought of solutions, and made cool contributions to the world of science and to our everyday lives. Are you the next?

Now, let your parents read this

This book can give you some excellent, creative, one-on-one time with your child. Even if you don't have a technical bent, you can help your kids with these projects because the directions are clear and straightforward, with explanations to help you understand the science and technology. Even children with short attention spans can be encouraged to make these projects—as long as they are given the opportunity to contribute.

Your contribution is important, too. Some of these projects involve using utility knives, electric drills, or hot-glue guns, so your supervision will be necessary. But you'll also contribute by brainstorming project variations with your child. The purpose of this book is to spur creative thinking in science and technology. Encourage your child to improvise. He or she may create the invention the world's been waiting for, and you'll have a great time trying together.

Perhaps most importantly, fight the temptation to skip ahead to projects toward the end of the book. The inventions presented here are arranged in a certain order, with concepts learned in one project built upon in later ones. Your child will get more out of the projects if you don't have to skip back and forth to figure out basic concepts before you take the next step.

The contest

One of the best things about this book is that it makes you think. Actually, even better is that you can get paid for thinking. Honest!

All of the projects in this book are interesting and they work. But you can make them even better by trying your own variations. If you think of something really good, you can enter the **Learning Triangle Press SciTech Invention** competition. You might even win first prize—$500 in cash! See the back of this book for your contest entry form.
And get ready to use your brain!

Symbols

The following are symbols used in the book:

Adult supervision

Requires adult supervision

Cool ideas!

Ideas for going further. Also, potential inventions for the Learning Triangle Press SciTech Invention Contest

Just-add-water

Version with off-the-shelf components

Make-it-from-scratch

Version using whatever's available; the creative inventor's paradise!

History/fun fact

Historical or other background info of projects

Scientific terms

Important terms being defined; can also be found in the glossary

Project 1

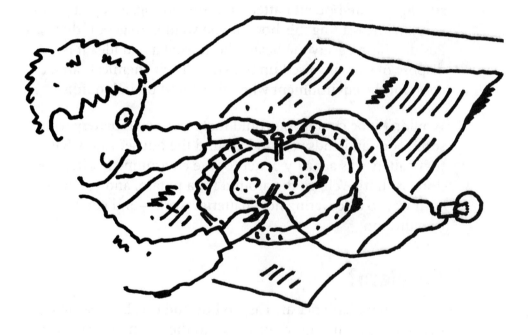

Power up!

ANY MECHANICAL DEVICE THAT YOU INVENT NEEDS A power source. For most of the projects in this book, that power source will be a battery. Think about it for a moment: How much money do you spend on batteries each year? You use them in toys, radios, calculators, clocks, remote controls, watches, and more. When you buy batteries at the store, you get a decent power source that is conveniently packaged and relatively cheap. Of course, you're not learning much about how things work by sticking a store-bought battery into something, and you probably wouldn't be reading this book if you wanted to get off that easy. Besides, hasn't everyone heard about what a bad idea it is to dispose of so many used-up batteries? Their chemicals aren't good for the environment when they wind up in landfills.

Wouldn't it be cool if you could make your own battery with some odds and ends you find around the house? And what if that battery was actually better for the environment when you're done with it? Well, go dig around for a potato, and you'll be on your way to discovering how batteries work—and you'll be earth-friendly, too!

Problem?

Store-bought batteries are easy to buy and use, but they're *too* easy for a great inventor like you, and they aren't very good for the environment when you throw them out.

Solution?

Make a battery from a few odds and ends that are biodegradable or can be reused in something else. By using different types of metals and by talking your parents into giving up one or more items from the fruit-and-vegetable group, you can construct an electrical power source. It will look crude and be pretty basic, but it will be disposable.

Science stuff

The main component in a battery is the *electrolyte*, which is the chemical medium that conducts electricity. Most store-bought batteries use alkaline as the electrolyte, but some use lithium and other chemicals. Your homemade battery contains an electrolyte, too—in this case, the natural electrolyte in all fruits and vegetables.

The other major components in a battery can be metallic or nonmetallic chemicals. Everyday 1.5-volt batteries (A, AA, and AAA) are made up of a zinc casing and a rod of carbon, with the electrolyte material in between. These two different chemicals react differently when exposed to an electrolyte.

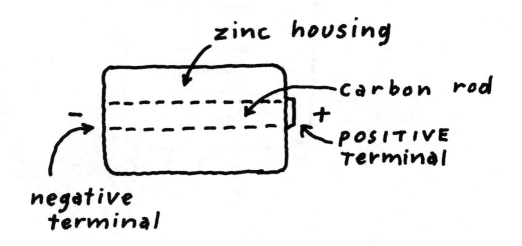

Battery history The type of electrical energy that comes from a battery is called *direct current*, or *dc*. The first battery was developed in the early 1800s by Alessandro Volta, an Italian professor and physicist. To honor him, the name *volt* has been given to that electrical force. *(If one of your projects makes it big someday, we might have to name an idea after you!)*

The first batteries were made up of a series of silver and zinc disks in pairs. The metals were separated by a *nonconductive* material, such as pasteboard. Then the whole assembly was submerged in salt water. When a wire was connected to the top disk of silver and the bottom disk of zinc, current flowed. These basic principles are still at work today in many of the batteries we use.

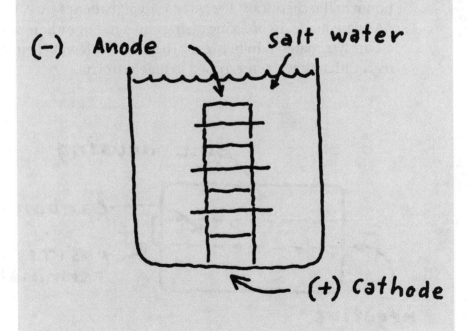

(−) Anode   salt water

(+) Cathode

The chemical reaction within the electrolyte attracts the negative particles in the carbon to the positive particles in the zinc. Because the carbon is releasing electrons (the negative particles), it is called the *anode* or *negative electrode*. The zinc is receiving the electrons, so it is called the *cathode* or *positive electrode.* When the two electrodes are connected to a light bulb, for example, the *circuit* is completed, and current begins to flow from one electrode to another. This current flow makes the light bulb work. The battery is "dead" when the electrolyte is used up.

Tips

You can use any fruit or vegetable for this project, but we'll refer to it as a potato throughout. Also, you don't absolutely have to have a volt-ohmmeter to make your battery, but it's kind of neat to be able to measure the voltage of your masterpiece when you're done.

Stuff you'll need

☐ 1 potato, lemon, grapefruit, or any other available fruit or vegetable

☐ 1 1.5-volt dc motor flashlight bulb or old digital LCD display (such as from a watch)

☐ 1 brass screw

☐ 1 steel pin, nail, or paper clip

☐ 1 24-inch length of insulated copper wire

☐ old newspapers

☐ foil pie pan

Project 1

□ wire cutters

□ sandpaper

□ utility knife

□ electrical tape

□ volt-ohmmeter (*optional*)

 How to do it

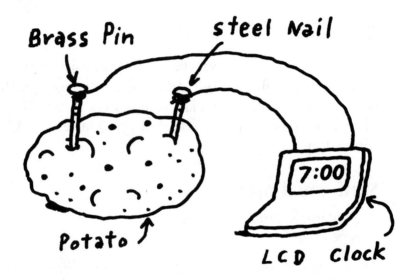

Brass Pin   steel Nail

Potato

7:00

LCD clock

1   Place newspaper over your desired work surface. Place the potato or the other fruit/vegetable in the foil pan.

2   Cut the copper wire in half, into two 12-inch lengths. Using the wire cutters, trim the insulation off 1 inch of each end of each 12-inch piece of wire.

3 Sand the steel nail (or paper clip) to remove any nonconductive sealant it might have. Wrap the end of one length of copper wire around the nail head. Insert the nail into the potato.

4 Repeat step 3, but use a brass screw with the other length of copper wire. Make sure the two metal pieces are close to each other in their potato home, but not touching.

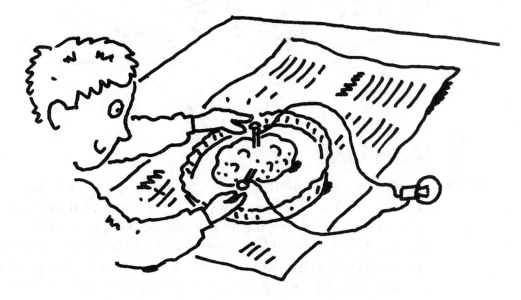

5 Wrap the two free ends of the copper wire to a flashlight bulb or to an LCD display. You might have to switch the *leads* (wire ends on the bulb) to get the current to flow properly.

6 If you have a volt-ohmmeter, use it to try to measure the voltage and current (dc) from the potato. See the illustration on the next page.

Cool ideas

As you can see, you can create a useful battery right in your kitchen. On the other hand, it's not a good idea to have aging potatoes and lemons lying around the house—and, really, it's hard to insert a potato into a wristwatch. So you're probably still going to want to use off-the-shelf batteries for most things. But understanding how batteries are made up and how they work will help you make the most of their use.

With more and more microprocessor-based electronic toys and devices available than ever, the voltage and current levels are within the realm of many fruits and vegetables. Maybe there is an electrolyte out there that can be both attractive and practical. Beyond just making a homemade battery, what other variation can you think of?

☞ What other materials could be used as a battery?

❀ Which materials would make a better electrolyte?

✷ What happens if you add voltage from another charged battery into the fruit or vegetable?

✷ What if you connect potatoes in series or in parallel, as shown? Do you get more voltage? More current?

☆ Besides making a potato-powered clock or flashlight, what else could you power with a more "natural" source?

Haven't we been using the same old batteries too long? Isn't it time for battery technology to leap? Somewhere out there is the long-life battery we all need!

Project 2

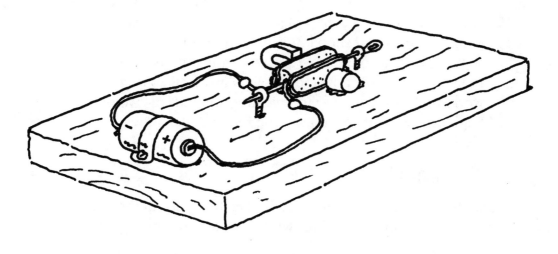

Get it moving!

DID YOU EVER THINK ABOUT HOW MANY DEVICES around your house are driven by an electric motor? Make a list, just for fun. First, there are the bigger motors: the dishwasher, washing machine, clothes dryer, vacuum cleaner, hand drill, circular saw, furnace, etc. If you move on to the smaller motors, you can count those in your VCR, CD player, hair dryer, and computer. It's amazing how many motors one home can have!

What do you do when one of those motors breaks? Chances are, you take it to a repair shop of some sort to have it fixed. The people at the repair shop know how motors work, so they have some idea what could be wrong when the motors aren't working. In fact, if you know how motors work and how to *make* one work, you're on your way to inventing all kinds of awesome stuff. So, inventor, what are you waiting for?

Problem?

Because motors power practically everything useful these days, you need to know how they work to create your own useful inventions.

Solution?

Build your own motor from scratch, and use it to make something move! By assembling your components the right way, you can construct a working model of an actual dc motor. *This will give you the basis for working with future projects in this book.*

Science stuff

Motors can run on *direct current* (dc) or *alternating current* (ac). The motors in your home—the ones that you have to plug into the wall—all run on ac. The best example of a direct-current motor is one powered by a battery.

With a dc motor, the scientific principle at work is *electromagnetic induction*. When an electric current passes through a metal, such as a pin or a piece of copper wire, it always produces a magnetic field. In this case, the electricity is directed to make the motor rotate.

Your dc motor will have four main components:

cork armature

field magnets

brushes

upholstery needle

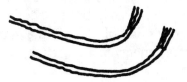

Project 2

1 *Armature* (a cork, in this case). This is the rotating part of the motor.

2 *Field* (magnets). This part of the motor stays still.

3 *Brushes* (two short speaker wires). The brushes bring electricity to the commutator (see below).

4 *Commutator* (some pins you'll put into the cork). Connected to the armature, the commutator rotates and picks up electricity as it turns.

Tips

The components for this motor are assembled on a workpiece known as the fixture. The fixture could also be referred to as a jig or a base, which are common terms for something used to guide a tool or to hold something still. This project's fixture is shown. You want a good, solid base and a stationary point for your rotating electric motor.

The early life of motors In the early 19th century, noted English physicist Michael Faraday concluded that forcing a change to a magnetic field would cause an electric field to be created. This has become the basis for most electric motors in use today. The phenomenon known as inductance is measured in units called *henries*—ironically named not for Faraday, but for another noted physicist, Joseph Henry. Faraday's unit of honor is the *farad*, used to measure the amount of stored energy in a capacitor.

Stuff you'll need

- ☐ 1 wood base, 6″ × 12″
- ☐ 2 eye bolts, at least ¾″ high
- ☐ 1 wine-bottle cork
- ☐ 2 large magnets, each with a north and south pole
- ☐ 1 long upholstery needle
- ☐ 2 1″ pins
- ☐ 1 battery holder
- ☐ 1 12-volt battery
- ☐ 1 24″ length of thin, insulated wire
- ☐ 2 6″ lengths of speaker wire
- ☐ 2 to 4 thumbtacks
- ☐ hot-glue gun
- ☐ wire cutters/strippers
- ☐ needlenose pliers
- ☐ electrical tape

Project 2

How to do it

1 Insert the knitting needle through the center of the cork.

2 Build the fixture base from the wood as shown, inserting the eye bolts so that the upholstery needle from the cork assembly will rest on each eye bolt.

3 Insert two 1-inch pins into one end of the cork. Cut two slots, down the length of the cork from each pin.

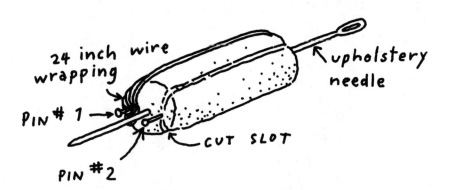

4 Wrap one end of the 24-inch length of wire around pin #1. Continue wrapping the wire around the cork, through the slots, to pin #2. Wrap the other end of wire around pin #2.

5 Set the cork assembly into the eye bolts. Locate one magnet on each side of the cork, and, using the glue gun, cement the magnets into position. See the illustration below.

6 With the wire cutters, strip the speaker wire ½ inch on each end of each wire. Using thumbtacks, position each end so that it "brushes" against its associated pin. (This will be the commutator and brush assembly.)

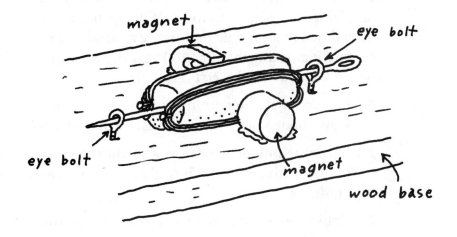

7 Connect the other ends of the speaker wires to the battery holder. Make the circuit as shown below, and secure it with electrical tape.

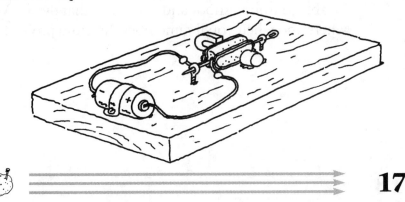

8 Insert the battery into the battery holder. The cork should begin rotating. (It might need a push to start it because even commercial electric motors demand high currents to start. Once running, their current requirements drop dramatically.)

SAVE YOUR MOTOR! You might be able to use it later in the book.

Cool ideas

Obviously, manufacturers of electric motors today have perfected Faraday's principle of electromagnetic induction, and they are improving its design even today. When you think about how many different ac and dc motors are around you every day, don't you find it amazing that this 100-year-old principle is still being used at the dawn of the 21st century?

☞ Can you make something useful from your crude motor? How about a fan or something else that rotates?

❉ Can you think of a better way to construct your project motor? Perhaps so that it could be enclosed and even used outdoors?

✳ Could you make a cool science-fair project from this example?

One day, you could be faced with a machine that's not working. Because you understand how an electric motor works, you might be able to troubleshoot and even "fix" that device. Who knows where and when you'll remember this little project!

Project **3**

In gear!

UP TO THIS POINT, YOU HAVE WORKED ON A POWER source in project 1 (the battery) and a prime mover in project 2 (the electric motor). But there's one more piece to the puzzle. You need to be able to control the power. You need a drivetrain.

Now, "drivetrain" might sound pretty intimidating, but basically what we're talking about here is a gear set. Through *gear reduction*, a gear set can control how fast the prime mover moves. Think about this: When you're riding your 10-speed bicycle, you're really using gear reduction to its max! The only difference between your riding a bike and building one of these projects is that *you* are supplying the power instead of an electric motor!

As you shift gears in your bike, something good happens that allows you to let the bike do more of the work for you. To go up a hill, you shift the bike's chain to gears so that your peddling is easier, but the bike's tires still turn enough to get you up that hill. On the other hand, when you want to go fast, you shift gears in the opposite manner. Well, this theory is used in almost every motor-driven device in the world! Gears make work easier.

Problem?

Once you give an electric motor its electricity, that motor wants to spin very fast, doesn't it? What if you don't want your device to rotate or turn that fast?

Solution?

You can use a variety of speed-reducing parts to slow the rotation to your device. As a matter of fact, by slowing the speed, you actually can turn a much larger or heavier object.

Science stuff

Many common household devices that we use run from an electric motor. This electric motor converts electrical energy into *mechanical energy,* which does the work. Fans, dishwashers, hair dryers, fish tank pumps, and other items do work for us. And you have probably noticed all the different parts within those appliances, especially when someone has taken them apart because they aren't working! There's the electric motor, sometimes a belt, sometimes a sprocket, and other times there are gears. These parts make up the *drivetrain,* the part of a machine that transmits power. This phase of the electrical-to-mechanical work cycle is called *power transmission (PT).* A drivetrain can be gears, pulleys, sprockets, chains, belts, or any combination of those things.

gear

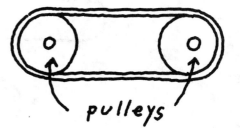

pulleys

sprockets

Project 3

A gear set can transmit power by itself, using only gears of different sizes and no other PT components. The scope of this project is to build a simple gear set, and the theory you learn here can be applied to other projects in this book. The best part is that you can actually reuse the gear box assembly you make in this chapter.

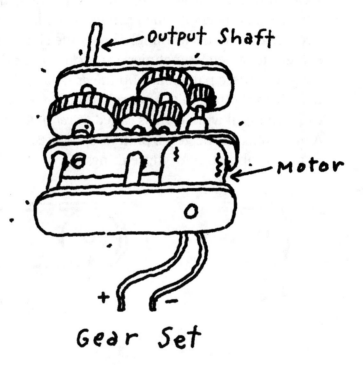

Gear Set

This project utilizes a battery-power source, a dc electric motor, and multiple drivetrain configurations. These configurations include different sizes and types of gears, and also include discussion for other possible attachments to the output of the gear set.

Dizzy dinners Have you ever seen one of those huge, rotating restaurants on top of a large building? Have you ever wondered how big the motor is that turns restaurants like those? They usually rotate very, very slowly, sometimes taking a whole hour to make a full revolution! But, if they rotated too fast, the patrons would get dizzy and sick—not a good idea for a restaurant. The amazing fact is that the electric motor driving a revolving restaurant with 100 people inside, is typically small—maybe only 15 horsepower . However, it runs through a drivetrain with a gear reduction of 120,000 to 1! That's a lot of gear reduction. In this case, gears help a lot!

For our projects, gear reductions are 40 or 60 to 1, adequate to run many future applications. The gear reduction of 40:1 means that for every 40 revolutions of the motor per minute, the output shaft through the gears turns *one* time.

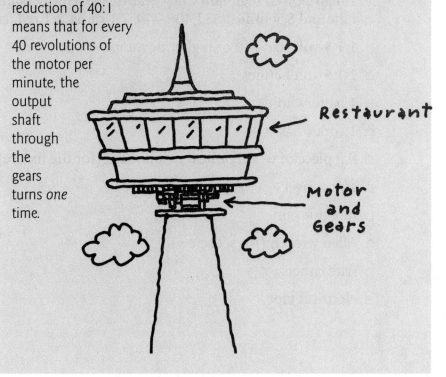

Restaurant

Motor and Gears

Project 3

The just-add-water version

You can find gear-set assemblies and plastic gears in toy and hobby stores, some hardware stores, and through some scientific products mail-order outlets. You might decide it's worth the $10 to $15 investment to purchase these if you intend to make some practical device. These purchased gears come ready-to-assemble, and you can secure them easily to a housing for your device. They also will have a framework to firmly mount the motor so that no slippage or backlash can occur. Your gearset will be more efficient, which is important for long life and extended wear.

Stuff you need

- [ ] 1 high-power, high-efficiency gear-box assembly (similar to an Edmund Scientific #S52,406—41.7:1 or 64.8:1 reduction)
- [ ] 1 1.5-volt size 140 or higher dc motor
- [ ] 1 1.5-volt battery
- [ ] 1 battery holder
- [ ] 1 cork
- [ ] flat piece of wood or heavy cardboard (for the fixture)
- [ ] screwdriver
- [ ] hot-glue gun
- [ ] Allen wrench (for set screw)
- [ ] wire cutters
- [ ] electrical tape

How to do it

1 Assemble the gearbox set as instructed.

2 On a suitable fixture, mount the gearbox set using a hot-glue gun.

3 Mount the battery holder to the fixture.

4 Cut the wires at the battery holder appropriately, and connect them to the dc motor. Wrap the connection with electrical tape.

5 Insert the battery to be sure the motor runs. Remove the battery.

6 Make a black mark on one end of the cork. Attach the cork to the output shaft so that the black mark is dead center.

7 Reinsert the battery. By keeping your eye on the black mark, count the revolutions at the output shaft. With known gear reduction, calculate the base speed of the motor.

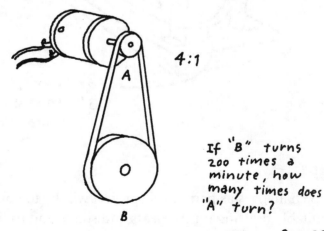

4:1

If "B" turns 200 times a minute, how many times does "A" turn?

Answer : 800 RPM

8 Change the gear reduction and repeat Step 7.

The make-it-from-scratch version

Depending on what items you can find around the house, you can make a simple drivetrain. A motor and battery will still be necessary. As for the gear reduction, you can use a belting arrangement with pulleys. Gears usually need to be used in conjunction with chains or other gears, and pulleys are used typically with belts. Either way, the reduction is still commonly referred to as *gear reduction*. As you can see, one pulley attaches to the motor shaft and another (twice the diameter will mean a 2:1 reduction and so on) will have to be connected to another shaft.

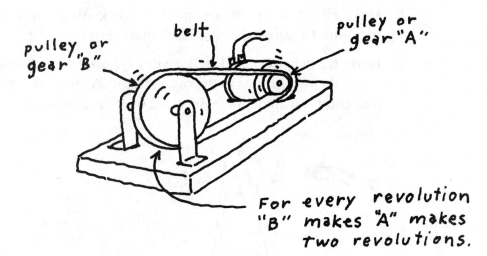

pulley or gear "B"

belt

pulley or gear "A"

For every revolution "B" makes "A" makes two revolutions.

Tips

Two challenges as part of this project will be to come up with a suitable housing for the gears and shafts and to find and use items from around the home (in the basement, attic, etc.) as the drivetrain parts. Old, discarded toys might contain gears and pulleys, and belts can be found in many mechanical products (old sweepers, older answering machines, tape players, etc.). Take a look around the house for these items and get permission from your parents before tearing something apart!

Stuff you'll need

- ☐ 1 1.5-volt battery
- ☐ 1 1.5-volt dc motor
- ☐ 1 battery holder
- ☐ 1 pinion gear, or similar small, tight-fitting plastic hose (This can be omitted if the gear that fits onto the motor shaft is tight enough.)
- ☐ 1 larger-diameter pulley
- ☐ 1 hard-rubber belt (a rubber band won't work; you can use leather, though, or even a flexible wire)
- ☐ 1 wooden fixture
- ☐ 1 wooden or steel rod (to use as a shaft)
- ☐ 2 small wooden blocks (to use as shaft bearing units)
- ☐ hot-glue gun
- ☐ wire cutters
- ☐ utility knife

How to do it

1 Using the hot-glue gun, mount the battery holder onto the wooden base.

2 Attach the smaller pulley to the motor shaft with hot glue.

3   Near the battery holder, locate and mount the motor with the hot-glue gun. Be sure that glue does not interfere with any electrical connections.

4   Make a lengthwise notch into the top of each wooden block.

5   Mount the blocks with the hot-glue gun.

6   Insert the rod through the larger pulley, and secure it with a small amount of glue.

7   Wrap the belt around the small pulley and the large pulley, and glue the rod/pulley assembly onto wood blocks.

8   Insert the battery, and watch it run!

Cool ideas

Any machine, big or small, that has movement probably utilizes an electric motor. Unless the motor directly drives the load (direct drive), then there must be some drivetrain components. Mastering which components to use and where to mount them comes with experience. Also, a secure mounting is necessary for proper, extended operation. With these thoughts in mind, what loads can you envision being driven by our homemade drivetrain? Some of these projects will follow in later chapters and you will want to reuse your gear box set. Other variations you might want to consider:

☞   What happens when you change the gear configuration to a speed-*increasing* situation instead of a speed/gear-reduction situation? Do you think it is harder to turn something faster?

✿   Do you have any old toys that might contain some gears? Are your parents throwing out any motorized appliances? Take them apart (with your parents' permission and supervision, of course), and use the drive components (any belts, gears, pulleys, etc.) for future projects.

✳ You can add gears to a system instead of changing the diameter or teeth configuration in an existing power transmission system. Try this with your existing setup.

✳ Can you make your own gears? Pulleys? Belts? What other household appliances contain these small components?

✩ The addition of gears also can affect the direction of rotation. Sometimes this is desirable, or even necessary. Can you think of a reason to do this? Try it and see what happens!

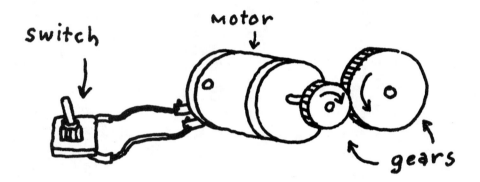

☞ To start and stop your motor and drivetrain system, you will need to add a switch so that you don't have to insert and remove the battery each time you want it to run. Where would you locate the switch?

These assemblies are the basis for many upcoming projects. You now have a power source, a prime mover (motor), and a drivetrain. With these items, you can run virtually anything. Start looking at devices that you see in stores and use your "X-ray" vision to understand how they are being driven. Recently, I purchased a motorized lollipop turner. The manufacturer had put a motor, battery, and gears into a plastic housing to turn a lollipop. I paid $4 for a 25-cent lollipop because I just had to see what was inside. But I did get a battery, motor, and gears. This proves that any invention has the chance to succeed, so start tinkering!

Project **4**

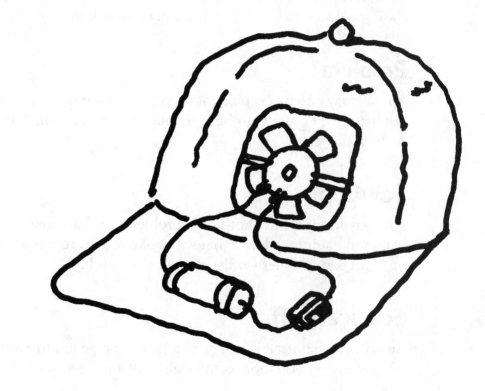

Put a fan in your hat

PICTURE THIS: IT'S A HOT SUMMER DAY, AND YOU WANT to go play outdoors with your friends. You need to keep the sun out of your eyes, so you grab a hat. But an all-star inventor like you doesn't wear just any hat out to play. Think of the impression you'll make on your sweaty friends when they see you cooling your brain with your latest invention—a working, battery-operated fan that you've installed in a favorite hat. Not only will you *look* cool, you'll feel cool, too. And it's really no sweat to create!

Problem?

An everyday baseball cap might keep the sun out of your eyes, but it also will cause your head to retain body heat, which will make you sweat.

Solution?

One way to solve this "hot-head" problem is to turn any common hat into a device that will make you more comfortable on a hot day. In other words, put a fan in your hat!

Science stuff

An ordinary hat itself is a *static* object. To change it into a *dynamic* device to make you more comfortable, all you have to do is *mechanize* it.

A *static* device is one that has no moving parts. It is at rest, and nothing is moving. A *mechanism* can be described as the working parts of a machine. A fan is made up of two distinct mechanical parts, a motor and a blade. Together, they are a mechanism. Once you add a mechanical part, such as a fan, to a static object, such as a hat, you've made a simple machine.

The fan for your hat has to be powered by some energy source and controlled by something. For this project, a battery will supply the power. A battery converts chemical energy into electrical energy. To control the power source (or to start and stop the flow of electrons to the fan motor), you will need a switch. The illustration shows a single-line electrical diagram of the switch, power source, and fan motor.

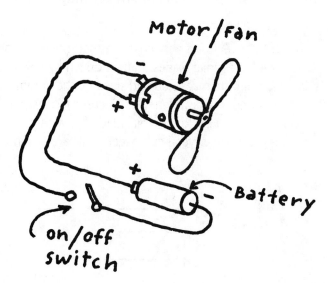

Tips

Select a hat you're comfortable using and wearing, but also be sure that it's one you want to alter. Where you want to put the fan is an important consideration. Not only do you have to ask yourself where you want the cool air to come from, you also have to decide what part of your hat you want to use. Keep in mind that you might not be able to see the hat's design or logo once you've installed the fan.

Be sure that the fan is blowing air onto your head, and not sucking hot air away. Sucking the hot air away might seem like a good idea at first, but unless you have a crew cut or have your head shaved, it will suck your hair into the fan. Eeeeooooowwwwcch! Also be sure that the fan is solidly mounted in your hat and that it has screens or your hair or some miscellaneous body part might get caught in the fan blades!

History A *fan* is a mechanism that moves or stirs air. Many fans have multiple radial blades that are driven by electric motors, steam, or gas. They are measured and sized by the volume of air they move. This volume of air is referred to as *cubic feet per minute* or *cfm*. As you can see, an enclosed radial blade fan with a large enough electric motor can move several cubic feet of air every minute. Of course, the fan you will use in your hat is much smaller, but it will provide a slow, steady stream of air—perfect for those hot summer days!

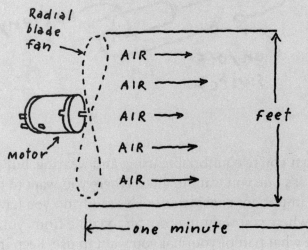

The just-add-water version

You can put a fan in your hat in no time at all if you start with a ready-made fan assembly. These days, smooth-running, quiet "micro fans" come fully enclosed and wired, and they are easy to find, thanks to the computer industry. Because computers generate so much heat, their insides contain small fans that circulate the air and cool things off so the computer doesn't literally burn out. You can purchase these micro fans through Radio Shack or Edmund Scientific. Of course, buying an assembled fan will cost more than buying the separate motor and blades and enclosing them (see "from scratch" version, p. 37).

Tips

This version of the fan in the hat will cost less than $15, provided that you already have the appropriate tools. If you can find a 1.5-volt fan and motor, the cost will be almost half as much. Of course, if you use a 1.5-volt motorized fan, you'll need to use a 1.5-volt battery. The good news is that 1.5-volt batteries are less expensive and easier to find than 12-volt batteries.

Stuff you need

- ☐ 1 baseball cap with reinforced front portion

- ☐ 1 micro fan, 12 or 1.5 Vdc, 250 mA (Edmund Scientific part #S39,091 or equivalent)

- ☐ 1 battery holder (Radio Shack catalog #270-405A or equivalent)

- ☐ 1 12-volt or 1.5-volt dc battery

- ☐ 1 single-pole, single-throw (SPST) switch

- ☐ hot-glue gun

Project 4

□ soldering iron

□ solder with resin core

□ wire cutters

□ utility knife

□ electrical tape

□ colored pencil (color should contrast hat color)

How to do it

1 After you have decided where you want your fan to go, place it on the hat in the desired position. Trace the outline of the fan onto the hat with the colored pencil.

2 On a surface suitable for cutting, cut the hat along the traced line with a sharp utility knife.

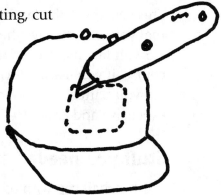

3 Place the switch and the battery holder where you want them on the fan. Determine how long you need each wire to be, and cut each wire to the desired length.

4 Either solder or tape the wires to each other and/or their termination point. A solid, firm connection is very important. HINT: Remove the battery from the battery holder so that the fan does not run constantly while you are soldering.

5 Place all the components on the hat in their final positions.

6   Using either a hot-glue gun, needle and thread, or clips, attach the fan assembly firmly onto the hat. (The glue gun will give you the best results.)

7   Reinsert the battery into its holder. Turn the switch to the ON position, and watch the fan run!

The make-it-from-scratch version

For those inventors who don't mind doing a bit more work, saving some money, and trying something different, the following version is the way to go. This version differs from the "just-add-water" version mainly in that you have to build up a fan-and-motor assembly from whatever you can find around the house.

Tips

You can buy a small, 1.5-volt dc motor for about 99¢ from any toy, hobby, or model-train store. You can also order what you need at Radio Shack, Edmund Scientific, or American Science and Surplus (addresses and phone numbers found in the back of the book). This type of motor will be a little noisy and will run rougher, but it will be much less expensive than the 12-volt variety. Again, if you use a 1.5-volt motor, you also can use a less expensive 1.5-volt battery (AA type).

The fun starts when you have to look for a suitable fan blade or propeller, which can be thin plastic (I used a bendable ruler that I didn't need anymore), wood, or even hard cardboard. When you find the blades, consider what type of housing you want to place around it. A perfect home for the fan blades is the top cover off an aerosol can, but if you use one of these, you'll have to have an adult drill air holes in it and help you attach it to the motor with a hot-glue gun. You will have to attach the blades themselves to the motor shaft.

Stuff you need

- ☐ 1 baseball cap with reinforced front portion
- ☐ 1 miniature dc 1.5-volt motor, with leads (if you can't get one with leads, you will have to solder your own on)
- ☐ 1 1.5-volt battery (AA size)
- ☐ 1 AA-size battery holder, with leads
- ☐ 1 fan blade (make out of plastic, wood, cardboard, etc.)
- ☐ 1 housing for the fan blade and motor (aerosol can cover)
- ☐ 1 SPST slide switch (or any adequate switch you can scavenge)
- ☐ power drill (might be necessary for drilling holes in housing)
- ☐ hot-glue gun
- ☐ electrical tape or soldering iron
- ☐ hacksaw, Dremel tool, or utility knife
- ☐ needlenose pliers
- ☐ wire cutters
- ☐ colored pencil

How to do it

1 For this version, attach the fan assembly on the brim of the hat to direct the flow of air toward your face. With this approach in mind, locate all your materials.

2 Have an adult drill air-inlet holes in the aerosol can top (the housing) as shown. Then, cut the top of the aerosol-can lid to the desired angle so that fan direction is appropriate.

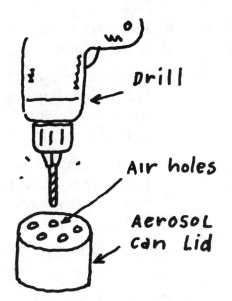

3 Cut the plastic, wood, or cardboard blades to a width and length that will fit within the housing without extending beyond the front edge. Securely attach the blade, bending or cutting it to get the best air-flow scheme.

4 Firmly attach the wires to the dc motor, making sure they will be long enough to route to your battery location.

5 Slide the motor into the housing, and pull the wires through one of the drill-holes in the back.

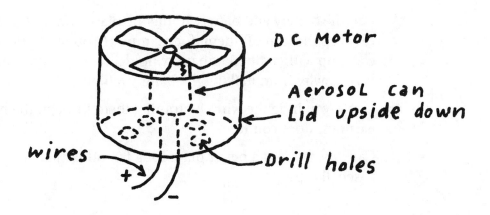

6   Using a glue gun or Super Glue, glue the motor onto the back of the housing.

7   Place the completed fan assembly on the brim of the hat. With a colored pencil, trace around the housing perimeter, then cut out along the tracing. Glue the housing onto the hat brim with the glue gun.

8   To one side of the housing, place the battery holder. Place the switch on the other side. Route the wiring as shown on page 33. Make sure all the connections are secure to and from each component.

9   Insert the battery, and turn on the fan. Stay cool!

Cool ideas

As you can see, there is more than one way to put a fan in your hat. Depending on what can be found around your house, you can change the final assembly's looks and location. Remember, being creative and resourceful is the idea behind this whole book. What variations of this project can you dream up?

☞ What other device, besides a fan, could you place in a hat to perform some useful purpose?

❀ Can the battery and battery holder be placed under the brim (to keep the rain off them, for example)? You might need to come up with a different battery holder for this variation, to keep gravity from making the battery fall out!

✳ Could you hide the wires by routing them through the hat? Neatness does count!

✩ Can you think of a better place for a fan other than a baseball cap?

Project

Pump it up!

EVERY SCHOOL HAS AT LEAST ONE DRINKING FOUNTAIN. In fact, no matter how many fountains your school has, after a hot gym class, it *seems* like there's only one! You're dying of thirst, but you have to wait your turn, and every kid in line in front of you seems to take an hour to sip that cool, refreshing water...but when you finally get your turn, it's worth it.

Wouldn't it be cool if you could make your own fountain? Even if making a drinking fountain doesn't appeal to you, have you ever considered how many different fountains are around us? Almost every city has a decorative fountain somewhere—in a mall, a park, or even in people's yards. Did you ever wonder what makes the water come up? And what makes it go back down? If you could figure that out, you could invent all kinds of "refreshing" projects and amaze everyone you know!

Problem?

You'd like to make a decorative miniature fountain to impress your friends. But how do you get the water to go up? And then how do you make it come back down?

Solution?

Water will go up if it is *pumped* up. And, if you know anything about gravity, you know that what comes up, must come down. This chapter deals with moving fluids—creating something pretty (and impressive) at the same time.

Science stuff

Early fountains took advantage of natural springs, which bubble up out of the ground and "pump" the water to a higher elevation. Gravity then forced the water back down, and as the water fell over rocks and sculptures and stuff, it created a soothing sound and a work of art.

Narrow orifice

But you don't need to find a natural spring to make a fountain. You can use an electrical pump and a network of pipes to move water. The electric motor will drive a set of *impellers*, or internal blades, which will move the fluid from one position to another. A *centrifugal* pump forces water under pressure through a narrow passage, which produces a bubbling and jetlike effect—and you have your fountain!

When you submerge the *intake* of the pump in water, and then use the motor to rotate the impeller blades, the water will begin to move. The moving water will try to find the easiest path it can find, which in this case is the outlet of the pump. The water rises out of the pump outlet and then falls back down, to be sucked back up the pump by the impellers, and so on. This is called a *recirculating pump system*. Whenever water is pumped up, it must overcome gravitational pressure called *head pressure*. If the water is pumped too high for the size of the pump, the flow will be very slow or even nonexistent. (See the illustrations on the next page.)

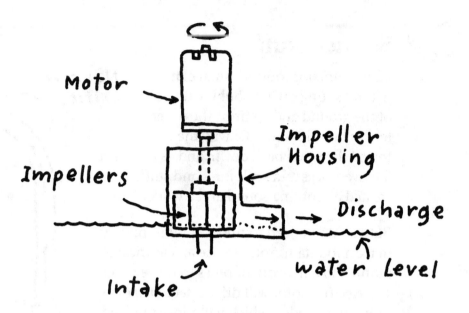

Motor

Impeller Housing

Impellers

Discharge

Intake

water Level

Water, water, everywhere Fountains can be found all over the world. Because water has a cooling effect, especially when falling, fountains are more common in the hotter climates. Because decorative fountains are considered works of art, many of the designers were famous architects, artists, and sculptors.

The first decorative fountains appeared on the scene about 5000 years ago in ancient Greece. But perhaps the best examples of fountains can be traced to ancient Rome. The Romans were exceptional at creating waterways, viaducts, and other water- related structures. Today, there over 300 fountains in Rome, each with its own story and legend.

The just-add-water version

Your decorative fountain can have whatever look you want. This version uses rocks in conjunction with colored lights.

Stuff you'll need

- ☐ 1 metal or plastic pan, 12″ wide × 2″ to 3″ high × 18″ to 24″ long.

- ☐ 1 miniature water pump with dc motor (Edmund Scientific part # S50,345 or equivalent)

- ☐ 1 1.5-volt battery

- ☐ 1 12-volt battery

- ☐ 1 1.5-volt battery holder

- ☐ 1 12-volt battery holder

- ☐ several rocks, mix of round and flat

Project 5

- 2 lengths of plastic tubing
- 1 set of 12-volt lamps (red, yellow, and green)
- 1 half-gallon of water
- hot-glue gun
- wire cutters
- electrical tape

How to do it

1 Secure the battery holders to the outside of the pan. Be sure you place them in locations that will allow you to reach the lights and motor conveniently. (You might want to try out the pump and lamps in different places in the dry pan to get those locations.) Use the hot-glue gun to securely fasten the battery holders.

2 With the hot-glue gun, secure the pump to the base of the inside of the pan. Make sure you don't cover up the water-intake section of the pump.

3 Run one length of the plastic tube from the pump outlet up and through rocks. Pile the rocks in a volcano-like configuration.

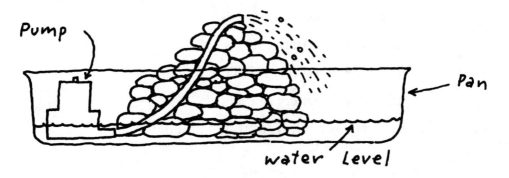

4 Route the other piece of plastic tubing through the rocks near the top opening. This will be used for the lights and as conduit for the wire to the lights.

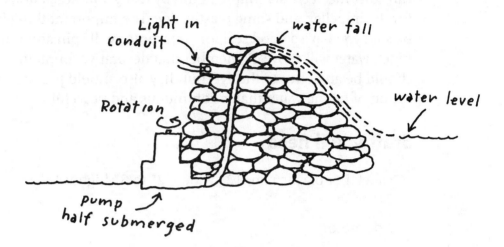

5 Connect the motor wires to the 1.5-volt battery holder.

6 Connect the lamp wires to the 12-volt battery holder.

7 Fill the pan with 1" of water.
NOTE: Do not completely cover the pump motor with water. This will cause the motor to fail.

8 Insert the batteries, and watch the fountain water fall.

9 Adjust the rocks and lights to get the best-looking (and best-sounding) display. The lights will show up better if the room is dark.

Tips

You can extend battery life if you wire more than one battery in parallel. On the other hand, you can run a larger motor if you connect the batteries in series. (See project 1)

The make-it-from-scratch version

Because the water pump is such an important component, you can construct a crude, simple pump by using a motor, a housing for the impeller, and some plastic pipe. The important thing is to be sure you have a good seal, or your motor will spin and not much water will move. Remember that decorative fountains should be attractive to the eye, but they also should produce a sound of falling water that is continuous and peaceful.

Stuff you'll need

- ☐ 1 metal or plastic pan, 12" wide × 2" to 3" high × 18" to 24" long

- ☐ 1 dc motor

- ☐ 1 1.5-volt battery

- ☐ 1 12-volt battery

- ☐ 1 1.5-volt battery holder

- ☐ 1 12-volt battery holder

- ☐ plastic material for impeller blades

- ☐ housing for motor

- ☐ switches (*optional:* You can install switches if you don't want to insert and remove the batteries every time you want to start and stop the pump and lights.)

- ☐ several rocks, mix of round and flat

- ☐ 2 lengths of plastic tubing

- ☐ 1 set of 12-volt lamps (red, yellow, and green)

- ☐ 1 half-gallon of water

- ☐ hot-glue gun
- ☐ wire cutters
- ☐ electrical tape
- ☐ drill
- ☐ utility knife

Tips

The more-resourceful inventor can build a pump from scratch. You'll need a dc motor as the prime mover, and you can make the impeller blades from any plastic material. Finding a suitable housing might be a challenge, but it's also half the fun. Your housing must be round and mostly watertight. It also has to be something that you can modify to include intake hole and an outlet. (You need to have an adult drill and cut the appropriate inlet and outlet holes.) You can make the housing airtight with the hot-glue gun after the impeller blades are inserted.

If you're really feeling creative (or you don't feel like spending any more money!), you can improvise even further by taking a plastic milk jug and cutting the top off with a pair of scissors so that you end up with a small plastic pan.

After you've built your own pump and housing, you can follow most of the steps from the just-add-water-version fountain.

Cool ideas

Throughout this project, we've talked about pumps as devices that move water. Of course, pumps can move many different fluids—and they can even move air in a compressor or air-pump scheme. For example, you can use a miniature pump as an aerator for a fish tank. In this setup, air is being displaced from one position, outside the tank, to another position, the inside of the tank.

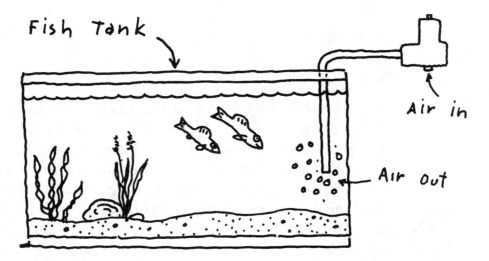

Fish Tank

Air in

Air out

Note: Remember that a pump used to move water uses that water to cool itself. When you move air with a pump, be sure that your motor is not getting too hot. If it does, you might need a bigger motor.

Another project that involves a water pump is an automatic houseplant-watering device. What a great gift for mom or dad—just make sure it looks good and isn't too hard to use. You can see in the illustration (see the illustration on the next page) how to set up the water pump with an on/off switch to pump the water into the plant. This setup could even be more elaborate if you add a timer and relay to the circuit to automatically trigger the water pump to come on. It's possible . . . It just depends on how inventive you are!

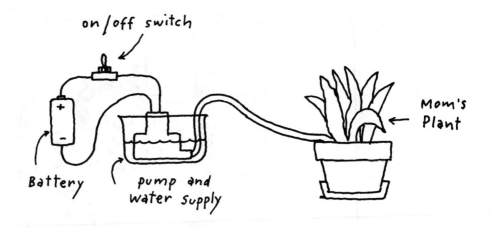

on/off switch

Mom's Plant

Battery

pump and water supply

If you *really* want to experiment, build a pump that can be fully submersed into a liquid (such as Kool-Aid), and you'll have a great drink dispenser. Shown here are a couple of approaches to this variation. One thing to keep in mind: If you attempt this idea, make sure that all your components are clean and washable.

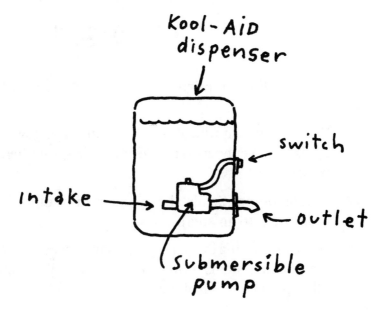

Kool-Aid dispenser

switch

Intake

outlet

Submersible pump

Other things that you might try with a pump and/or fountain project:

☞ You can run multiple pump fountains along with multiple lights for a very decorative fountain (a great science fair project, too).

☆ A water pump can also be used as a humidifier (putting moisture into an area).

✳ By incorporating switches, and maybe even timers, you can make your systems more automatic. Can you think of any other possible control ideas?

Project  6

Jewelry-go-round

DID YOU EVER TAKE A GOOD LOOK AT A JEWELRY BOX?
Not an empty one, but one with loads of chains, earrings,
necklaces, and bracelets in it. Even if you don't have one yourself,
you've probably noticed that most jewelry boxes aren't very good
at keeping jewelry organized and untangled. When you think
about it, the whole point of even having one is to store jewelry in
a organized way until someone's ready to wear it. If you have to
dig around in piles or untangle everything before you wear it,
what's the use?

A cool jewelry box is a small merry-go-round. That's right, the
merry-go-round that you ride at the amusement park is what you
need—minus the horses, of course. A miniature version of that
carousel could show off any collection—jewelry, pogs, baseball
cards (science project books?!)—as well as being a practical,
organized storage system.

Problem?

Your jewelry box (or someone's) is a complete mess—tangles of
bracelets and necklaces and chains all over the place.

Solution?

Build and motorize a "jewelry-go-round" that will keep any
number of pieces tangle-free, neat, and easy to find. And, if you
make it as a gift for Mom, you'll be praised and adored for your
ingenuity (and maybe even get out of doing chores for the day . . .
it's worth a try, anyway!).

History The first merry-go-rounds or carousels can be traced back to 17th-century France. The French word *carousel* referred to a popular tournament that featured men dressed in horsemen costumes, with fun and games following the contests. The Tuileries Gardens in Paris is the site where a carousel was given by King Louis XIV in 1662. This is called *Place du Carrousel*, the place of the carousel.

Much like this carousel project, the first merry-go-rounds and many other amusement park rides actually started as small-scale models. The story goes that a toymaker in France set hobby horses on a platform and rotated it, at first by hand. This toy was developed because, at that time, only nobility could enjoy the magnificent, full-scale versions. As the attraction of the miniature merry-go-rounds grew, they were then built larger to accommodate many people.

The just-add-water version

Much like the amusement park rides, the prime motor for our project will be a dc motor. However, our motor will operate on 1.5 to 6 volts dc, and amusement park motors are several horsepower and run from voltages of 230 or higher. What happens if the motor is connected without any gears? It runs very fast, right? You will have to reduce the speed to your carousel or it will fly off the table. Using gear reduction will ensure that there is enough power to turn the carousel at slower speed—even when it is loaded with all your jewelry.

Tips

As you can see, the jewelry carousel could get top-heavy, so you will have to add some weight to the base. This extra material will also help to hide—and even mount—the motor. Remember as you design and build that neatness counts! If your project works *and* looks good, others will be impressed. In our society, packaging and looks sell thousands of products that are otherwise pretty basic and even dull. The selling price of these well-packaged products is even higher!

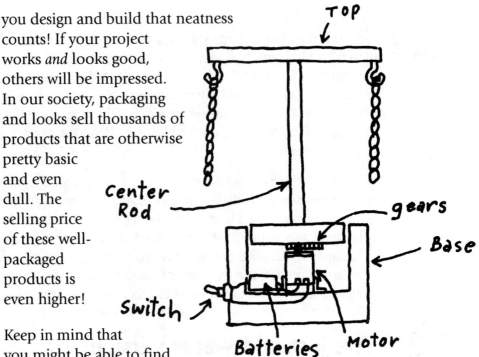

Keep in mind that you might be able to find existing assemblies to incorporate into your project. If you're a good inventor, you've probably already learned where to dig up inexpensive, motorized, miniature toys. Of course, inside these toys are motors, gears, and sometimes even a good battery with a switch. If you can find something like this, your work is over halfway done.

Just-add-water version

Stuff you need

□ 1 dc motor with integral gear set (similar to the one shown on page 22)

□ 1 battery to match motor

☐ 1 battery holder

☐ 1 pushbutton switch

☐ 2 identical plastic plates, 5" to 6" diameter, to fit within coffee-can housing (light, soft plastic works best)

☐ 10 cup hooks (or as many as you want to place around the top plate)

☐ 1 7" to 8" length of ½" diameter wooden dowel rod

☐ 1 half-height coffee can (2 lbs. or less, 6" or 7" diameter)

☐ 1 2" × 4" block of wood (for weight, and to attach the motor/gear set and battery to)

☐ hot-glue gun

☐ spray paint

☐ saw

☐ electric drill

Tips

If the specified coffee can is not available, an old, square jewelry-box bottom will do. You'll just have to fit a round peg into a square hole!

How to do it

1   Spray paint your plastic plates, center rod, and can or wooden housing the color of your choice.

2   Have an adult help you cut the 2" × 4" block to fit down inside the bottom of the can housing. This will add weight to the base.

3 Attach the motor and gear set, shaft-up, to the base. Secure with the hot-glue gun.

4 Have an adult drill a hole in the can housing to run the wires through. Wire to and mount the switch with glue to the outside of the can housing.

5 Set the battery holder(s) securely in place on the wooden block. Connect all the wires to and from the battery and switch.

6 Glue the wooden block to the bottom of the can housing. This portion of the jewelry-go-round will be stationary. The rest of the assembly will rotate on the motor shaft.

7 Select one plate to be the top plate. Glue the cup hooks to the underside of the top plate. If they can be screwed in safely (with no exposed screw points), use that approach.

8 Glue the center rod to the top and bottom plates respectively. This now is the rotating portion of your jewelry-go-round.

9 Drill a small hole in the underside of the bottom plate. Then glue the entire rotating portion to the output shaft of the motor/gear set.

10 Place some chains and bracelets on the cup hooks, insert a battery, and flick on the switch!

Make-it-from-scratch version

If you want to save money or get more creative with the design of your jewelry-go-round, you should consider using more wooden pieces for plates, housing, etc., cutting these (with adult supervision, of course!) to the size and style you like using a jigsaw. You could also add a lightbulb, or incorporate an area on the top side of the bottom plate for rings, posts, earrings, and so on.

To utilize the cam principle mentioned earlier in this project, consider using a cam to pop up a "secret" box, housed below the bottom plate. Through a cutout in the bottom plate (maybe with a light cover or door), the secret box could come as the jewelry-go-round rotates, displaying your collection of really "fine" jewelry!

Cool ideas

You might be used to looking at amusement park rides as something cool you stand in line for and have fun on. But the amusement park is full of motors, controls, and machinery. The next time you're waiting in line at the amusement park, take a good look at how that ride is being controlled. Look at the motion. Does the ride go up or down? Does it rotate? Is there a motor? Gear reduction? Before you get on that ride, understand how it works (and maybe decide whether or not you think it is safe!).

Just as the toymaker in France made a scaled-down version of a merry-go-round so that common people could enjoy it, so can you develop a device the world might enjoy one day. That toymaker's invention became more than a reality. It was built into a large-scale amusement park ride, and the poor guy probably never even got to ride on one. So get moving! You might be able to invent the next amusement park ride (and even live to ride on it)!

☞ What kind of a ride would you enjoy that doesn't seem to exist now?

✳ Think of the need first. How about a storage container for CDs, videotapes, and game cartridges? Some exist but can you improve them? Motorize them?

Science stuff

You've probably noticed that on an amusement-park carousel, some of the horses do not move up and down, while many others do. The principle at work is that of the *cam*. A cam is a mechanical piece, shaped in such a way that it can yield a certain type of desired motion. The cam is an integral part of many toys and appliances we use every day. In fact, there is a *camshaft* in every automobile engine; this rotates and moves the engines pistons in a correct order, timed to the firing of the spark plugs. Without the cam, your daily activities certainly would be different!

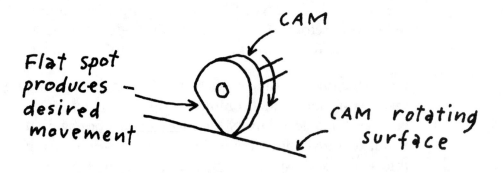

CAM

Flat spot produces desired movement

CAM rotating surface

Your carousel does not have to incorporate a cam unless you want one. Where would you install it? If you wanted to get fancy, a cam could be attached to a special compartment on the carousel which only "pops" up once every revolution. This compartment could hold your rings.

Need a shine, mister?

YOU PROBABLY KNOW THAT SHOES CAN SAY A LOT about you. What do they say? Well, they don't actually talk (even though they do have tongues!), but they can tell people about your tastes, your habits, even your favorite sports. It's not just the *kind* of shoes you wear; it's also what condition they're in. If your shoes are neat and attractive, it shows you care about how you look. That might not matter to you too much now, but later on in life you'll go on your first job interview, and you'll *have to* care about how you look. Shiny shoes might not get you the job, but dirty, scuffed, falling-apart shoes could severely hurt your chances. Potential bosses might think that if you don't care about your shoes, you won't care about the job.

Even though you might not have a lot of reason to wear dress shoes now, many grown-ups (whether they're looking for a job or they already have one) have to have clean and shiny shoes every day. Imagine how proud your parents would be if you surprised them with shiny shoes one morning.

Here's the best part: You actually could make a little extra money if you learn how to shine shoes properly. In hotels, airports, train stations, and on city streets, you can find shoe-shine vendors, shining and buffing the shoes of travelers and business people for a fee. They do it by hand, with clean cloths and a lot of elbow grease. But imagine how many more shoes you could shine (and how much more money you could make!) if you had a motorized shoe-buffer.

The shoes that said too much An escaped criminal once got caught because of his shoes. This crook had escaped from police custody, and he ran away to the airport. In a men's room there, a friend had hidden some money and some clothes so that the criminal could disguise his appearance, hop on a plane, and make his escape. When this bad guy came out of the restroom, he was dressed in an expensive suit instead of his jail clothes—but he had forgotten to change his shoes! His old, ratty shoes were so out of place with the rest of his outfit that one of the cops noticed it, and they caught him! In this case, his shoes had said too much about him.

TERMINAL C ⟹

Problem?

You'd like to break into the shoe-shining trade with an invention that will shine shoes in a new, different, and better way.

Solution?

Build a motorized shoe-shiner and buffer, and shine your way to success!

A walk through shoe-shine history

If you're going to shine shoes for a living, you'd better learn how! It really is something that should be done right; people will notice if you do a sloppy job.

Over three thousand years ago, sandals were the common protective footwear. From these early sandals, hundreds of types of shoes have evolved—from sturdy work boots to fancy dress or dancing shoes to high-top basketball sneakers. Most shoes are made from leather and usually are fitted with a rubber heel. Just as shoes protect our feet from dirt, rocks, rain, and snow, they need to be protected with a coating or two of shoeshine polish.

The illustration labels a standard shoe to help you learn the different parts you'll be shining and buffing. You probably didn't realize that there was this much to know about shoes. Those shoe salespeople sure do earn their money!

Begin by cleaning any loose dirt from the shoe's *heel* and *outsole*, then make sure the *welt* is free of any dirt. Next, put the actual polish on the *vamp* and the *backstay*. Rub the polish into the shoe and wipe the residue off. Now it's time to *buff* the shoe. This final stage of the process puts the high-gloss, shiny finish to the shoe's surface.

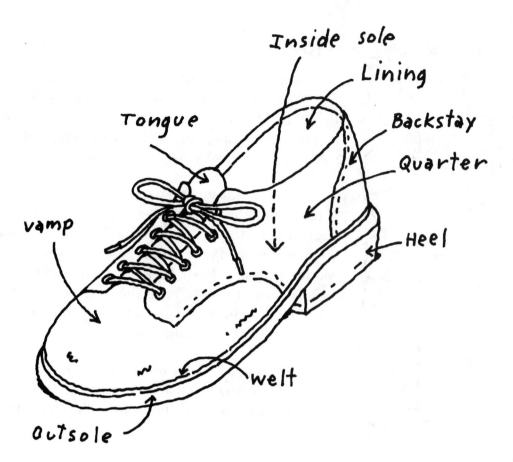

Inside sole

Lining

Backstay

Quarter

Tongue

Heel

vamp

welt

Outsole

Science stuff

The handheld shoe buffer, when completed, will spin the "buffing-head" thousands of revolutions per minute. This will allow you to shine a shoe nicely and even get into some "tight" locations . Keep in mind that the motor has only so much *torque-producing* capability. You are not introducing any gear reduction (which would yield more torque) because you want a high-speed operation to get the shiny finish you (or your customers) will desire.

Tips

This project involves using available household items, a dc motor, battery, a switch, and even an optional lightbulb. The handheld shoe buffer can be a great surprise gift because you don't need much parental supervision or involvement to make it.

The shoe buffer features a reusable buff material and is mainly intended to be used just to buff the shoe. Keep in mind that if you press too hard on the shoe when you're using the buffing tool, the spinning motion will slow down. Back off when this happens. A light touch when buffing is the secret. That's why you should still apply polish and remove it by hand to extend the life of the buffer.

Of course, if you're really inventive, you might come up with some alternatives that let the machine do *all* of the work. Some other "cool" ideas are at the end of the chapter.

The buffing of shoes is a good, practical application for this project, but you could also use it to buff and shine other items in the house. For example, your small buffer could do a nice job on jewelry once it is cleaned. Jewelers apply special creams to their gold and silver, and then they need to buff it off to get a bright finish. Of course, the buff material should be very clean (no black shoe-polish remnants!), so you might want to reserve one buffer assembly for jewelry only and the other for shoes. You can even ask your parents what other items around the house they want polished.

The just-add-water version

Actually, this project is relatively easy to put together, but it does use some elements of the "from scratch" idea, since you'll be scrounging around for the perfect housing (the spice or prescription-pill bottle housing, for example).

Stuff you'll need

- ☐ 1 small plastic container with a twist-on cap. A plastic spice bottle or even a prescription bottle will work well.
- ☐ 2 corks
- ☐ 1 soft, clean cloth rag suitable for good buffing of shoes.
- ☐ 1 1.5-volt dc motor
- ☐ 1 1.5-volt (AA) battery
- ☐ 1 AA battery holder
- ☐ 1 on/off switch
- ☐ electrical tape
- ☐ light wire
- ☐ hot-glue gun
- ☐ utility knife
- ☐ drill
- ☐ wire cutters
- ☐ white all-purpose glue (such as Elmer's)

Project 7

How to do it

1 Cut two strips of the cloth to a size that will wrap around a cork.

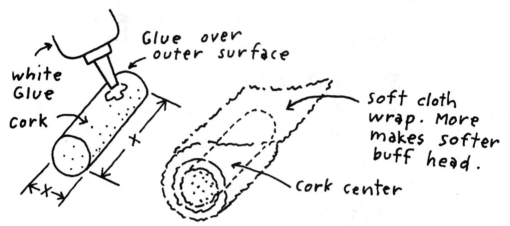

white
Glue

Glue over
outer surface

cork

soft cloth
wrap. More
makes softer
buff head.

cork center

2 Apply a thin, even coating of glue onto each cork's surface. Wrap each cork with cloth, and let them dry for one hour. The second cork will be your spare. Once the buff material on one cork is dirty and worn, you can cover it again with another strip of cloth, or you can replace the whole cork assembly with your spare.

3 While the corks are drying, cut out the bottom of the plastic container with the utility knife. What was the bottom of the container will become the back end of your buffer assembly, where you can access the motor and wires (see the illustration on the next page).

4 Have an adult drill a hole in the twist-on cap, big enough to allow the motor's shaft to go through.

5 Using the hot-glue gun, affix the motor to the cap with its shaft through the hole in the cap. Make sure that the shaft still spins freely.

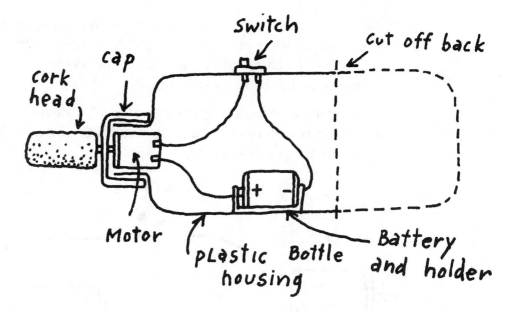

6 Have an adult drill a hole in one end of each cork assembly, at the exact center. This hole must be deep enough and big enough to accommodate the motor's shaft.

7 Mount the cork assembly to the motor shaft with glue. (Using a glue like Elmer's, which is soluble in water, will allow you to remove the cork from the motor shaft later if you want to replace it. Simply soak the cork in hot water for a bit, and it should slide right off.)

8 Take another look at the entire buffer assembly that labels all the pieces (see the illustration above). Mount the battery holder and switch in the rear of the plastic container as shown. (Leave the battery out of the battery holder for now.) Use the hot-glue gun for this.

9 Pull the motor wires through to the back, and screw the cap supporting the motor onto the remaining plastic housing.

Make sure that there is plenty of wire length coming off of every component—enough so that all the wiring can be pulled out the back end of the housing and so the connections can be made rather easily.

10 Attach each wire to its proper mating wire. Secure the connections with electrical tape, and stuff the wire carefully back into the plastic housing.

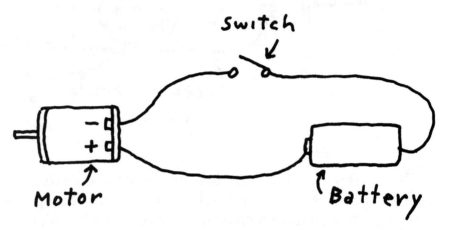

11 Insert the battery into the battery holder, flip the switch, and go put some shoe polish on a pair of shoes!

The make-it-from-scratch options

You've had a chance to catch that creative spirit in this project by using things around the house (the spice bottle or medicine container, and maybe even the corks) to make a useful project. If your object is to improve on this project, you could modify it for a specific purpose. For example, by attaching a small, 1.5-volt flashlight bulb to the plastic housing, you can power it from the same battery on board. You can focus this light toward the work surface so that you can see exactly what you're shining and buffing. This will be especially helpful if you choose to make a jewelry buffer instead of a shoe buffer because you'll be able to see all the tiny curves and crevices in rings and earrings.

You could spray-paint the housing and make a cover to hide the wiring and motor. Remember, the packaging of the project can affect its usefulness—as well as what other people might think of it. If it looks sloppy, they might not think it's such a hot item. On the other hand, you might want to make one of these buffers for your parents or for friends. In that case, you'll definitely want it to look great.

Of course, if your object is to save money, the best "from scratch" option is to make as many parts as you can yourself. You can, of course, make a motor yourself instead of buying one (see project 2). Be sure the homemade motor and housing will fit within the buffer container.

Cool ideas

☞ What if you applied a sticky material to the buffing head? You could make a motorized lint-picker-upper.

❇ Keeping the motor, power source, and housing the same, can you think of any other heads or attachments that would perform a different task?

✳ What if you changed the size of the motor? A larger motor with a matching power source could go into a bigger housing (a bigger plastic bottle) and could support a larger head.

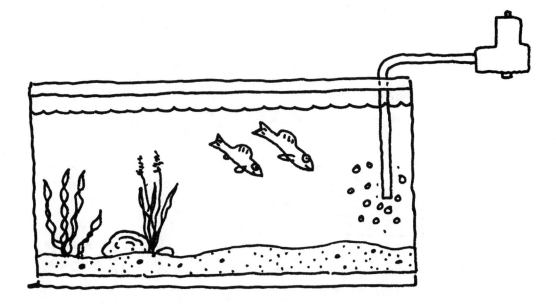

School lunch

IT'S FRIDAY AFTER SCHOOL AND YOUR FRIENDS WANT YOU to go camping with them until Sunday. Your parents say yes, which is really cool because the rest of your family will be visiting boring relatives all weekend. You're all ready to roll up your sleeping bag and head out the door when it suddenly occurs to you: Who will feed your fish? The last time you asked your neighbor...well, it wasn't pretty. You've got to come up with a way to feed your fish from the campsite. Hurry! Your friends want to know if you're going with them. Tell them you'll be there. But you'd better get started on solving the school (of fish) lunch problem now!

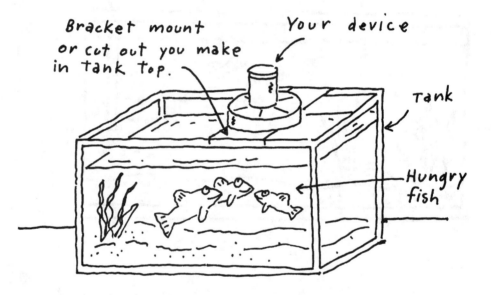

Bracket mount or cut out you make in tank top.

Your device

Tank

Hungry fish

Problem?

No one's going to be home to feed your fish. You're fond of these finned friends so you want them to eat, but you really want to go camping with your human friends, too.

Solution?

Build and install an automatic fish-tank food dispenser to allow you to have fun while your school of fish has lunch!

Science stuff

Engineers, scientists, and inventors all create because they need something for some purpose. They started with a problem, too. Your problem, of course, is that you want to feed your fish without having to be there. You've decided you want to build an automatic feeder, so you have the solution to the problem. Now you have to work backwards to figure out how to make your project. This is sort of a version of *reverse engineering*. Ask yourself questions like:

☞ How big should the food compartment be?

❧ What principle can you use to get the food to the fish?

✳ What kind of power source do you need?

✳ When do the fish need to be fed? Do you need a timer of some sort?

✮ Where will this mechanism mount on the fish tank?

Once you've asked and answered all the relevant questions, you can begin to solve your problem.

Project 8

Tips

One of the secondary problems with this project is that of controlling the motion properly. The solutions are to start and stop the motor *electrically* at the appropriate times or to gear the motor *mechanically* (as it runs continuously) so much that the compartment door moves ever so slowly, gradually letting food fall into the tank.

Stuff you need

- ☐ 1 dc motor
- ☐ 1 ac-to-dc converter, 110 volts ac to 6 volts dc or less (sometimes called a *power supply*, similar to those used for charging car phones, answering machines, etc.); should have adjustable dc output
- ☐ 1 digital timer (Radio Shack #61-1060 or similar); one you can set for seconds is best
- ☐ 1 plastic sinker container with individual compartments
- ☐ 1" × 4" metal strip (to make a Z shape)
- ☐ black electrical tape
- ☐ miscellaneous wire
- ☐ utility knife
- ☐ white glue or hot-glue gun
- ☐ electric drill

How to do it

1 Sketch out your plan as shown, customizing it to your fish-tank setup.

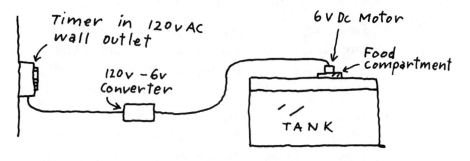

Timer in 120 v AC wall outlet

120v – 6v Converter

6 V Dc Motor

Food Compartment

TANK

2 Assuming your fish tank has a cover (if it doesn't, have you noticed any of your fish flopping on the carpet?!), you must make a small hole, approximately ⅜ inch in diameter, in the plastic cover. This will allow the food to fall freely from the sinker container as it indexes over the hole.

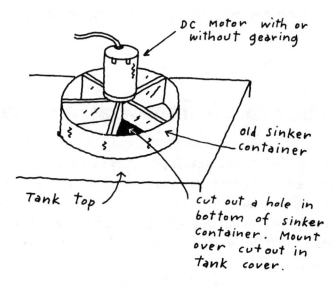

DC motor with or without gearing

old sinker container

Tank top

cut out a hole in bottom of sinker container. Mount over cut out in tank cover.

3 Next, have an adult drill a small hole in the sinker container to mount the dc motor's shaft. When the motor is in place, secure it with glue.

4 Set the sinker container assembly over the hole in the fish-tank cover. **Do not glue it to the cover!**

5 Bend the metal strip into a Z shape. This will act as a "torque arm," keeping the motor secure but allowing the sinker container assembly to rotate, or *index*. Fit the strip so that it can be glued both to the motor and to the tank cover.

6 Now for the electrical control stuff: Take the ac-to-dc converter, and cut the jack off the end of the wires. Connect these two wires to the appropriate terminals of the motor. Wrap them with electrical tape.

7 Plug the timer into the wall outlet, and plug the ac-to-dc converter into the time.

8 Fill the compartments of the sinker container with fish food.

9 Set the timer to come on and off quickly to index the container over the hole in the tank cover and allow the food to drop.

10 Go camping!

The make-it-from-scratch version

Digital timers are somewhat expensive, so you might decide to use a mechanical (less expensive) method to solve your problem. Some motors are built with gearing within, so the output of the motors is very slow—$\frac{1}{10}$ or less revolutions per minute. You can use one of the analog appliance timers found around your house and one of these "timing motors" for your project. You'll get the same result—for less money!

Stuff you need

- [ ] 1 dc motor with built-in gears, $\frac{1}{10}$ RPM output, sometimes called a *timing motor* (American Science and Surplus #22223 or equivalent)

- [ ] 1 ac-to-dc converter (110 Vac to 6 Vdc) to match your motor

- [ ] 1 analog appliance timer

- [ ] 1 plastic sinker container

- [ ] utility knife

- [ ] white glue or hot-glue gun

- [ ] 1″ × 4″ metal strip

- [ ] miscellaneous wire

- [ ] black electrical tape

- [ ] electric drill

How to do it

Follow steps 1 through 10 from the just-add-water version. Simply substitute the analog timer and the timing motor. Set the analog timer, and make the necessary adjustments with the timer. An analog timers doesn't have the accuracy that a digital timer has, but that's why you're using the slow-moving timing motor in this version!

Cool ideas

How could you apply this same concept to other things around your home? A stripped-down version could merely have a pushbutton and battery for the motor, which you could turn on any time you need to feed your fish. Imagine—no more fish-food-smelling fingers from "pinching" the food out of the jar! What other alternatives can you think of?

☞ Could the dog or cat dish somehow be set up to feed your other pets automatically?

✳ How could you reduce the basic cost of the unit you built in this project?

Project **9**

All mixed up

HOW MANY TIMES A DAY DO PEOPLE STIR A DRINK IN your house? Do your parents put cream and sugar in their coffee or honey in their tea? Do you like to drink Kool-Aid, instant hot chocolate, or chocolate milk? Of course, spoons work nicely for this kind of mixing, but spoons are so . . . BORING! Since you've become an inventor, you want to motorize everything you see. Your kitchen probably contains an electric mixer of some kind, but conventional electric mixers and beaters are much too large to fit into a cup or a glass.

Wouldn't it be cool to have something that could stir up a drink in no time flat without resorting to a boring, old spoon?

Problem?

You have to mix different kinds of drinks a gazillion times a day, and a spoon takes too long (and it's ho-hum boring, too).

Solution?

Make a battery-operated drink mixer to hang near the kitchen sink, ready to stick right into the liquid any time you want a cool, refreshing, quickly-mixed-up drink! By cutting and modifying items that normally get thrown into the garbage, you can make something useful to everyone in your house (see the illustration on the next page).

Science stuff

This project is similar in principle to the automatic shoe buffer (pages 63 to 73), but it has one major difference. Just like with the buffer, this project transmits the dc motor's *speed* and *torque* directly through the cork coupling. This will allow both projects plenty of power to spin (and buff or mix). However, while the mixer can be handheld and can do a great job of mixing many types of drinks, it will not be powerful enough to mix heavy powders, syrups, mashed potatoes, and so on. Of course, you can always experiment with more power . . . !

The just-add-water version

For this project, keep in mind that the mixer housing for the switch, motor, and battery should be plastic. The actual stirrer or mixing blade can be a plastic swizzle stick or stirrer. These should be easy to come by (and they're very inexpensive), but you could always try your hand at developing a plastic stir-stick with actual blades, like a real mixer. Or you could make a poor old plastic spoon less boring by using it on the end of your mixer contraption.

You will be using a small cork as the coupling from the motor shaft to the stirrer. The cork is a good choice because it's easy to adapt to just about any stirrer you want to try.

Stuff you'll need

☐ 1 small plastic container with a twist-on cap (A plastic spice bottle or an old prescription bottle will work well.)

☐ 1 1″ long cork

☐ 1 clean swizzle stick, hard-plastic straw, or plastic stirrer

☐ 1 1.5-volt dc motor

☐ 1 1.5-volt (AA) battery

☐ 1 AA battery holder

☐ 1 on/off switch

☐ electrical tape

☐ light wire

☐ hot-glue gun

☐ utility knife

☐ drill

☐ wire cutters

☐ white all-purpose glue (like Elmer's)

How to do it

1 Cut out the bottom of the plastic container with the utility knife, as shown. What was the bottom of the bottle will become the back end of the housing for the motor-and-battery assembly. Cutting off the bottom of the container will allow easy access to the components.

2 Have an adult drill a hole in the twist-on cap, big enough to allow the motor's shaft to go through.

3 Using the hot-glue gun, affix the motor to the cap with its shaft through the hole in the cap. Make sure that the shaft still spins freely.

4 Have an adult drill a hole in each end of the cork, at the exact center. This hole must be deep enough and big enough to accommodate the motor's shaft on one end and the plastic stirrer on the other.

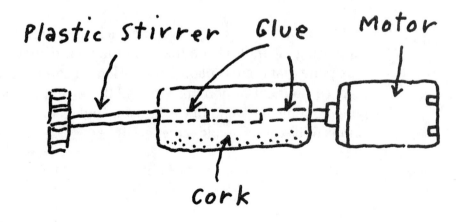

5 Mount the cork assembly to the motor shaft with glue. (Using a glue like Elmer's, which is soluble in water, will allow you to remove the cork from the motor shaft later if you want to replace it. Simply soak the cork in hot water for a bit, and it should slide right off.)

6 Glue the plastic stirrer piece into the other end of the cork.

7 Take another look at the exploded view of the entire mixer assembly that labels all the pieces. Mount the battery holder and switch in the rear of the plastic container as shown. (Leave the battery out of the battery holder for now.) Use the hot-glue gun for this.

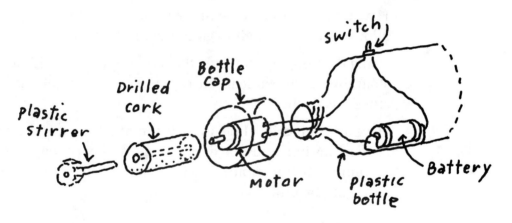

9 Pull the motor wires through to the back, and screw the cap supporting the motor onto the remaining plastic housing. Make sure that there is plenty of wire length coming off of every component—enough so that all the wiring can be pulled out the back end of the housing and so the connections can be made rather easily.

10 Attach each wire to its proper mating wire as shown. Secure the connections with electrical tape, and stuff the wire carefully back into the plastic housing.

11 Your final assembly should look like the illustration on the next page. Insert the battery and go make some hot chocolate! Don't forget the marshmallows!

The make-it-from-scratch version

By reusing items you've found around the house, you've made some elements "from scratch" already, adding to creativity and keeping your costs down. This is definitely a good thing! The bad thing is that if your device doesn't get used, nobody will think it's all that practical.

One way to ensure that people use your invention is to make it reliable and *handy.* Making sure that the batteries are good and that the cork assembly is solid will make it reliable. Making a mounting bracket for it and keeping it near the kitchen counter or sink (wherever you're allowed to keep it and wherever drinks are usually mixed) will make it handy.

When you embark on the mounting-bracket idea, again find the perfect discarded item in the basement or garage that you can turn into a permanent home for your mixer. Consider the areas you have to work with, and plan everything out on paper before you start sawing things up or tearing into the kitchen walls. A possible mount is shown, but the sky's the limit! (Come to think of it, the *ceiling's* probably the limit in your kitchen!)

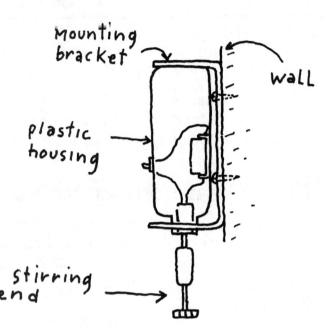

mounting bracket

wall

plastic housing

stirring end

Cool ideas

All in all, this project has as many other possibilities as your imagination can "stir" up. You might even want to ask your friends or parents what they would like in a device. Some other variations you might try:

☞ Make different mixer heads and attach them to other corks. Some drinks might get mixed better than others just by switching mixer heads.

✳ What will a larger motor and housing do for this project?

✳ Can you think of a way to make the motor and mixer run slower? Faster?

✳ How do you propose to keep the stirring end clean? Can you think of an invention to clean it? A better way to make it so that the stirring part can be easily removed for cleaning?

Project 10

Rotocones

HAVE YOU EVER NOTICED THAT MANY INVENTIONS have been developed because of convenience? They reduce the amount of work you have to do so you can kick back, and if you remember the M.O. of the inventor from the introduction of this book, you're supposed be spending your free time creating, inventor! OK, so you've loaded the automatic dishwasher for your parents, and the machine is doing the dishwashing work for you. You have the opportunity to create right now!

But you're a kid, so you decide to get an ice-cream cone instead. As the ice cream starts to melt, it oozes down over your hand on one side...and suddenly, you think of a problem you need to solve (and you were hardly even trying!).

Problem?

You want to enjoy a moment of daydreaming while you're eating an ice-cream cone, but the lick-and-rotate routine requires you to work too hard.

Solution?

How about a device that will continuously rotate an ice cream cone so that all you have to do is supply the tongue? Imagine the uniform and consistent lick you'll achieve on the ice cream while the motor rotates the cone evenly for you. Your cone will not only taste good, it will look good, too!

Today, machine designers and engineers work from an existing design and either improve it, modify it, or change it. They are almost copying the original design; they are *designing by*

replication. There is no harm in using available technology, products, and concepts to create something new and better!

Re-inventing the wheel
Ever since the invention of the wheel, C.E.s (Cave Engineers) and their successors have continually been improving on that original concept. Today, computerized machines and robots have evolved from that first wheel. Ironically, most motion in machinery is still focused around a rotating theme, much like that old, stone wheel.

The just-add-water version

This is one "just-add-water" project that requires you to be a little creative at the beginning in order to make your project go together a lot easier. You can find inexpensive, motorized toys and gadgets, many of which even have a battery, in practically any store these days—from the grocery store to the toy store to Wal-Mart or Target. If you can find these items at a good price, buy lots! You never know when you might have a use for them (like now!). You will probably notice, being the scientific observant type, that the motion of some these gizmos is slow...and that means you're getting a gearset, too!

I once found a lollipop turner that had a battery, dc motor, pushbutton, and worm gears in one complete assembly. It had been gradually marked down from $4.99 to $3.99, and eventually to 99 cents. At that price, I had to buy a bunch. If you tried to buy the individual parts, you would pay four or five times as much (and many small items are hard to find). Be on the look out for bargains and strive to get assembled components! The illustration shows a really nice assembly, all ready to go!

The next challenge is to find a shape suitable to place ice-cream cones into. Can you think of any plastic cone-shaped items you might find around the house? If you can't find something at home, try looking in a housegoods store. There are all kinds of cone-shaped plastic funnels, cups, and other stuff that could serve your needs. You might have to cut the plastic shape so that it will hold the ice-cream cone and fit onto the center rod that rotates the cone.

Science stuff

Because you're improvising on so many pieces of this project, you'll have to improvise your own specifications and assembly instructions, too. *Specifications* are the written description of the details for a project, including materials and types to be used, sizes, how they should (and shouldn't) fit together, and so on. Specifications for a building, for example, are usually legally binding and make up a major portion of a contract. Specifications writers are individuals who can think logically and methodically. They usually have some technical schooling and some project experience. Specification writers also can write product technical manuals and assembly instructions — providing that person has spent real time doing the assembly of the product.

Stuff you'll need

- ☐ 1 subassembly (from an old motorized toy or gadget) with motor, gears, pushbutton switch
- ☐ 1 cork
- ☐ 1 battery (to fit subassembly requirements)
- ☐ 1 plastic cone-shaped housing (cup, funnel, etc.)
- ☐ hot-glue gun
- ☐ white all-purpose glue (like Elmer's)
- ☐ wire cutters
- ☐ needlenose pliers
- ☐ utility knife
- ☐ heavy-duty scissors (able to cut plastic)

Project 10

☐ pencil and paper

☐ drill (optional)

How to do it

1   Once you have gathered your pieces, draw a quick sketch of your proposed invention, showing the parts as you have them. You might notice that you left out an important part or that you have a potential problem. Now is the time to work that out. Remember, it's always easier to change something on paper .

2   With the utility knife or heavy-duty scissors, cut the top of the plastic cone-shaped item to a shape to fit an ice-cream cone. Keep in mind that most people like to eat at least part of the cone when the ice cream gets down to a certain level. You'll have to leave enough of the cone exposed so the user will still get that satisfying "crunch."

3   If you're using a funnel, cut off some of the stem that protrudes from the bottom, and trim the cork with the utility knife so that it fits perfectly within the funnel's hole. If you're using a cuplike object, have an adult drill a hole in the bottom of the cup until it is big enough to accept the cork in a tight fit. It's better if the hole is a little small; you can trim and twist the cork into fitting, but you can't get back the lost piece of cup if the hole's too big!

4 Have an adult drill a hole in one end of the cork. This hole must be deep enough and big enough to accommodate the motor's shaft.

5 Mount the cork assembly to the motor shaft with glue. (Using a glue like Elmer's, which dissolves in water, will allow you to remove the cork from the motor shaft later if you want to replace it. Simply soak the cork in hot water for a bit, and it should slide right off.)

6 Place the cork into the hole in the bottom of the plastic cone holder. This must be a tight fit! When you have it just right, affix the cork, which is now attached to the motor assembly, with the hot-glue gun.

7 Find an ice-cream stand and show off to all your friends!

The make-it-from-scratch version

If you can't get your hands on a subassembly like the one described in this project, never fear! If you've completed any of the other projects in this book, you already know how to build an all-purpose motor, gear, and battery assembly. You'll need to think a bit about the perfect housing, but you can easily adapt a design from projects such as the jewelry-go-round (pages 53-61), the handheld shoe-buffer (pages 63-73), and the drink mixer (pages 83-90).

Many toys and products contain a motor and a battery. How many can you think of? How many are in your bedroom right now? How many are "retired" and in your attic, basement, or garage, collecting dust right now? If you have some old, discarded toys or gadgets in storage, you might want to resurrect them (put new batteries in) and begin tinkering with them. Take them apart. There probably will be some component in some toy that you'll be able to use for your next invention. Become a component and parts pack-rat. If you are serious in your inventing ways, you'll find a use for everything you find. Just make sure you have enough storage for your collection of parts!

Cool ideas

As you are quickly finding out, many inventions require a motor or means of moving something. Controlling that motor is called *motion control.*

☆ What if you came up with a way to stop the motor after it ran for a certain period of time (using a timer, maybe) or after it had performed its desired function (a limit switch or stop switch, for example)? Could you make the motor go in reverse?

✳ Why are dc motors used in place of ac motors? How could you modify these projects to ac?

Project 11

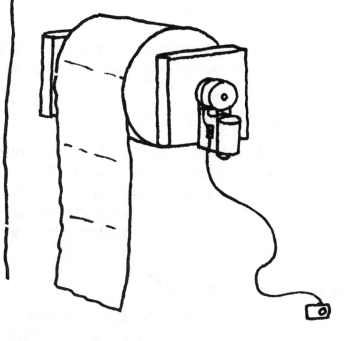

Power your TP with dc

HOW MANY TIMES HAS YOUR BABY BROTHER OR SISTER
unrolled the toilet paper and made your mother angry? Has your
cat ever gotten into the bathroom and completely unraveled the
entire roll of toilet paper? Have you ever tried to unroll some
toilet paper and the dispenser is stuck or hard to turn? Talk
about frustration!

Problem?

Someone always seems to mess up the toilet-tissue dispenser in
your house, and you're usually the one stuck trying to fix it.

Solution?

Make a dc-powered TP (toilet paper) dispenser! Invent a device
that is mounted higher than the conventional, traditional
dispenser, out of reach of toddlers and pets. A motorized toilet-
paper dispenser also will do all the work. It will turn the roll
easily and consistently while you hold down the *on* switch.

Science stuff

To complete this project, you'll have to use many of the
principles you've already learned in this book. A roll of toilet
paper might not seem too heavy to you, but it's heavy to a small
motor, so you will have to incorporate a gear set. The gear set
serves two purposes. First, it slows the rotational speed of the roll
as it turns. (If you didn't add the gears, the paper would dispense
very fast or get tangled and not dispense at all.) Secondly, by
reducing the speed, you increase the output torque, which is
the power that actually turns the roll.

Think about this: A full roll of toilet paper weighs much more than an empty roll, right? *You* know that, but your motor probably hasn't thought much about it. Always size your motor and gear set for the "worst" condition or load—in this case, the full roll.

Of course, you also need a power source for this project, which will be a battery. In this case, you might want to use two or more batteries. You don't want to have any dead batteries at the worst times, do you?

Tips

As you begin to look for the individual components for your automatic paper dispenser, think about a couple of things. First, the just-add-water version should use most of a pre-fab toilet-paper-holder's parts. In other words, if you can motorize an existing assembly, with minor alterations, then you have saved yourself a lot of time.

Seek out the "perfect" dispenser. It should be able to adapt easily to the addition of a motor and gearset. It also should allow you to change rolls from one end, the non-motor end. Finally, the roller assembly must be free-rolling—not a sticky, hard-to-turn roller. The illustration shows a nice, wooden tissue holder that has these features.

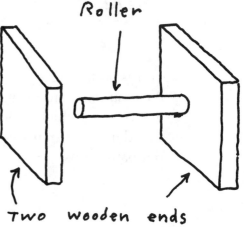

Roller

Two wooden ends
one end removable

Project 11

Two other very important tips: Be sure with mom and dad that you can mount this contraption in your bathroom (you are actually doing some home remodeling with this project)! Also, after you've installed your project, be sure that your parents buy the right kind of toilet tissue for your device. Tightly wound rolls are bad because static electricity in the room actually holds the individual sheets of tissue to each other. These rolls will not work.

History When you motorize a roll of tissue in your bathroom, you are actually replicating the original process that brought us the roll of TP in the first place! Large motors are used when toilet paper is made. As the rolls are wound and rewound at high speed, they are also under tension. This tension actually makes the roll tight and can determine how much tissue paper is on the cardboard tube, or *log*.

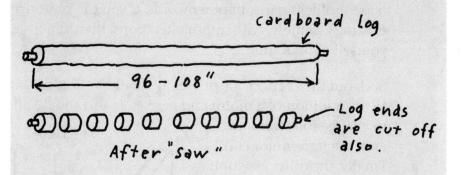

At this point, the log is very long. Some glue is applied to it, and the tissue sticks to the glue and is wrapped at high speed around the log. Next, the long log goes to a station called a *saw*. Here it is sawed into the many individual-size rolls that we end up with in our bathrooms.

The just-add-water version

Once you have found the perfect toilet paper holder, you'll still have to modify it a little to make it motorized. For starters, most holders let the roll of tissue sit loosely on the roller. One very simple method to make the roll stiffer for motorizing is to stuff heavy paper around the log and the roller, making them turn as one. The drawback to this method is that you will have to re-stuff the log each time you change a roll.

Stuff plenty of hard paper in here to stiffen Roller to Log.

Another method is to make a more permanent roller assembly. This can be done several ways, but one example is shown here. More upfront work for this one, but it makes it more practical!

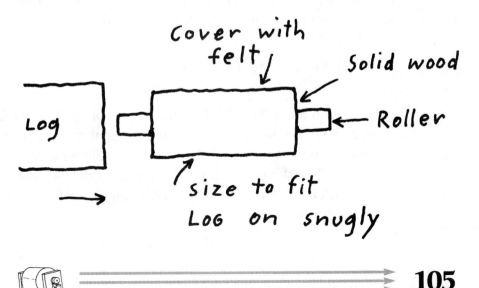

Cover with felt

Solid wood

Log

Roller

size to fit Log on snugly

Stuff you'll need

- ☐ 1 toilet tissue holder (preferably wooden)
- ☐ 1 1.5-volt dc motor
- ☐ 1 1.5-volt battery
- ☐ 1 battery holder
- ☐ 1 gearset
- ☐ 1 section of a 2 × 4 to mount the gearset, motor, and battery.
- ☐ 1 pushbutton switch
- ☐ wire
- ☐ hot-glue gun
- ☐ wire cutters
- ☐ electric drill
- ☐ electrical tape

How to do it

1 Study the illustration of the motorized dispenser. First, figure out how you can get the tissue roll and the roller to move as one unit.

2 Attach the 2 × 4 section to the TP holder as shown, using the hot-glue.

3 Next, you must do some layout and planning. Determine how you can place the various components so that the gear shaft can be inserted into the roller, while still allowing room on the 2 × 4 workpiece for the other pieces of the assembly. Have an adult drill a hole in the TP holder big enough to insert the gear set shaft.

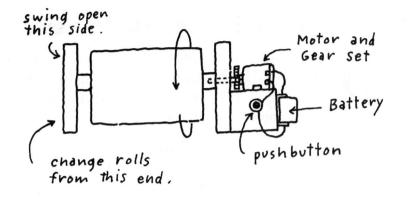

swing open
this side.

Motor and
Gear set

Battery

pushbutton

change rolls
from this end.

4 When you have mapped out your project and know that everything will fit, hot-glue the gear set shaft into the drilled hole in the roller.

5 Firmly seat the motor, battery holder with battery, and gear set onto the 2 × 4.

6 Following the wiring diagram, finish the wiring to and from the motor and battery(ies). Before you glue on the switch and wire it, think about where the best location for it might be. When you want paper dispensed, you will want quick, easy access to the pushbutton, so mount the switch on the dispenser somewhere where it will be easy to use. Complete the wiring.

7 Insert a battery into the battery holder, load the roller with some TP, and let 'er rip!

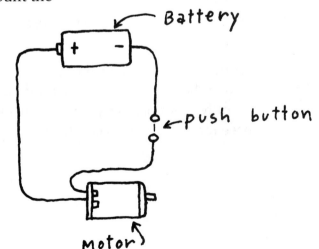

Battery

push button

Motor

Project 11

 The make-it-from-scratch version

Extremely creative individuals can create a customized, motorized TP dispenser totally from scratch! However, you will need some tools—such as saws and a drill—and you'll need a little adult supervision, too.

1 Put your design on paper first. Try to use full-scale dimensions, and don't be afraid to incorporate crazy ideas! Think fully how you will put the pieces together.

2 Get some 1"-thick board, and get an adult to help you start cutting out your design. A saber saw will do the job nicely—a scroll saw, even better. Remember to use safety glasses and let an adult do the hard stuff!

3 For a homemade roller, an old table leg cut to the right length will work great.

4 Once your pieces are cut, sand them off with sandpaper. Hot-glue them together, trying to be as neat as you can.

5 At this point you can either stain and varnish or paint the whole assembly, and allow it to dry. It might take a day or two

6 Now you are ready to repeat most of the steps in the "just-add-water version."

7 It might be nice to attach your pushbutton switch to a long wire so that the user can have maximum flexibility (and it will further "coolify" your project!). See the illustration on the following page for an example. Have fun!

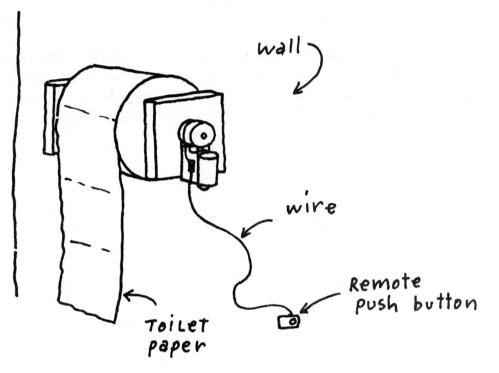

wall

wire

Remote push button

ToiLet paper

Cool ideas

Any paper product in the shape of a roll can be fitted with a motor if you want. For example, couldn't paper towels be unwound automatically? Some kitchens don't have a paper towel rack, so the roll just sits on the kitchen countertop near the sink. A motorized dispenser could work well in this kind of situation.

A really cool project, and one that will take a lot of thought, could be to somehow automatically dispense tissues from a box of tissues. This is a tough one, but it's possible. If robots can weld cars together, you can develop a gadget that grabs facial tissue! If you invent this device, I want you to send me one of the first ones (after you patent it, of course, and become rich and famous)!

Your brainstorming and thinking has to sometimes include the bizarre and off-the-wall thoughts. The idea that you might think isn't an idea could be the idea that actually leads you to the "perfect idea!" Start bouncing some ideas off of your friends. Then get them to help you *build!*

Project  12

Sun dogs

WHAT'S BETTER ON A NICE, SUNNY DAY THAN TO COOK hot dogs outside? Whether you're camping or just in your own backyard, nothing says "lazy summer day" like a plump, juicy hot dog cooked outside. Of course, usually, you have to rely on your parents to fire up the grill when *they* feel like it because they probably don't want you to mess around with the family Hibachi (or an open fire, for that matter!). But what if you could get the sunlight to cook those foot-longs for you? Then *you* could decide when to eat--and you might even get to be head chef!

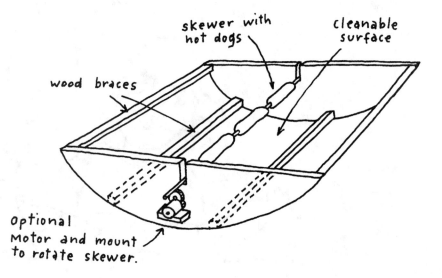

skewer with hot dogs

cleanable surface

wood braces

Optional Motor and mount to rotate skewer.

Problem?

You want to have a hot-dog cookout on a sunny day without relying on your parents, their grill, or an open fire.

Solution?

You can build a hot-dog cooker that not only cooks those juicy wieners clear through but also rotates them slowly—without matches! And the neat thing is that you'll never have to provide a new battery, and the cooker won't wear out. Your sun dogger will even be easy to clean!

Fun sun facts The sun provides, or has provided, all the basic energy on earth. Without sunlight we would not have coal, oil, or gas (*fossil fuels*) to produce any usable energy. The sun's rays allow for *photosynthesis*, which enables plants to thrive; when the plants die, they yield the fossil fuels.

More directly, the sun showers our planet with a tremendous amount of energy every day. Capturing that energy is the exciting field of solar energy, which is the emphasis of this solar hot dogger project.

Where's the best place to cook by the sun and when is the best time? The answers are multiple. The equator and the tropics get the most sunlight from our host Sun, which is some 93 million miles away. The best time is noon, when the sun is directly overhead.

Science stuff

Two principles of solar energy are at work in this project. One is called *photovoltaics,* the process of converting sunlight into electricity. The other is exploiting the *solar constant* to cook those juicy hot dogs. The total energy radiated by the sun for a given period of time and in some type of units is called the *solar constant.*

Project 12

For instance, did you know that, on a sunny day, every square foot of the earth's surface in that sunlight is receiving approximately 150 watts of energy every minute? That's a lot of power, and it's worth harnessing. If you concentrate that energy by reflecting it to the skewer on a solar hot-dog cooker, the actual temperature around the hot dogs will increase several times, allowing you to cook the hot dog the whole way through. This principle utilizes a geometric configuration called the *parabola* and is used in solar-energy-generating stations around the world.

The skewer on this hot-dog cooker is the *focus*, or *focal point*, which concentrates the sun's radiation toward the hot dogs. If this were not done, your hot dogs would not heat up enough to cook the whole way through. By constructing the hot dogger into the shape of a parabola, as shown, you can direct those rays to the focal point.

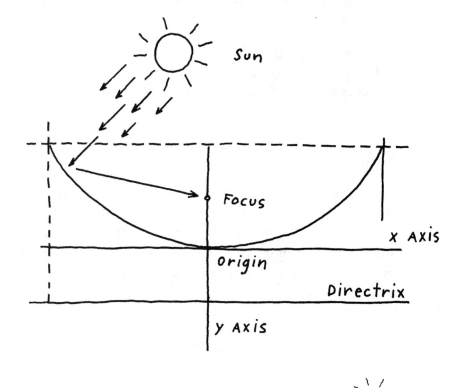

A *parabola* is a geometric shape evolved from a conelike, or conic section. It can be illustrated as a two-dimensional curve (see the illustration on the top of the next page). In this illustration, you can see why the parabola is the optimum shape for directing radiated light waves for that given area of space, either into the parabolic shape or out.

Parabolic shapes are important in many other items we use. For instance, automobile headlights are shaped as a parabola (see the illustration on the bottom of the next page) to radiate the light outward. A look at a flashlight will show you the same concept. The light waves are emitted from the concentrated source, the bulb.

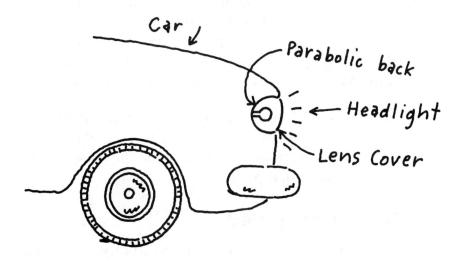

Converting the sun's rays to electricity, or photovoltaics, is done primarily today with silicon solar cells. A large surface area is required to produce a small amount of electricity. A 2×4-cm cell can deliver one-half of a volt direct current (dc) at 0.3 amps in full sunlight. Wiring cells in series allows for greater voltages, and wiring them in parallel yields higher currents. The dc motor turning the skewer can be run directly from the sun, too, using electricity created from solar cells to power your small dc motor. That motor turns the gearset, which turns the hot dogs on the skewer! (Of course, you can cop out and use a battery, if you want.)

The only version

Because this project is arguably the most complicated in this book, we'll stick with one version. You will have the choice of whether or not to add the photovoltaic motorized skewer, but, as always, you are encouraged to question, to experiment, and to let your ideas take you to new and better ways to do everything.

Because of the difficulty of this project, parental involvement will be necessary, but I'm convinced that you'll find this project the most rewarding, most educational, and the most fun of all the projects. Read on, if you dare...

Scope of the project

When you complete this project, you will have built, from wood and metal, a device that can cook hot dogs, sausages, or other meats by utilizing the direct energy from the sun. With that energy focused toward the meat, temperatures will be high enough to cook—without an open fire!

This project will require some sawing and some assembly, but once that's been completed, you can store your hot-dog cooker from season to season. (If your climate is sunny year-round, it might never be stored!) The cooker will be fairly bulky (the bigger it is, the more hot dogs can be cooked at a single time), but it will not weigh very much. With any solar-energy collection, a good deal of surface area is required to capture and concentrate the sun's heat. Your unit will have suitable surface area to capture that energy and its shape will concentrate that energy to gain cooking temperatures.

Note: One thing to keep in mind as you plan your solar hot-dog cooker is its shape.. The one shown on page 119 is a good choice. Others, as you can see below, are not as effective for collecting the sun's energy.

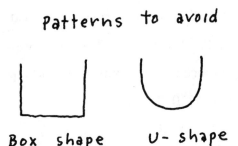

Patterns to avoid

Box shape   U-shape

Project 12

Stuff you'll need

Note: The sizes of many of the materials needed for this project can vary. Try to find materials as close to the size you need. This solar cooker will work just as well with items smaller or bigger than those listed. Simply make the necessary adjustments as you go.

- ☐ 2 1″ × 10″ × 20″ wooden boards (you may vary the length if necessary to match better with the available sheet metal).

- ☐ 1 36″ × 36″ piece of sheet metal with one side highly reflective (or whatever size you can find—we don't want to get into a lot of sheet metal cutting!).

- ☐ 1 lot of brads or tacks (one end sharp enough to penetrate the sheet metal and the head big enough to hold the metal in place once tacked)

- ☐ 1 38″ ⅛″-diameter steel rod

- ☐ 4 1½″ × 1½″ × 34″ long pieces of wood

- ☐ 1 lot of 1½″ Phillips-head wood screws

- ☐ 1 large piece of cardboard to use as a pattern

- ☐ 1 2″ × 4″ × 10″ block

- ☐ 1 wooden angular brace

- ☐ 1 gearset

- ☐ 1 1.5-volt dc motor

- ☐ 1 coupling, a quick-disconnect type on the skewer end

- ☐ 1 battery and battery holder *OR* 1 1.5-volt solar cell (similar to American Science and Surplus #11714 or equivalent built-up rating). *Note:* If the solar cell approach is used, then more horizontal surface area is required for the mounting of the solar cell. Remember, it must also face the sun!

- ☐ 1 switch
- ☐ electric variable-speed drill
- ☐ hammer
- ☐ drill bits and screwdriver head
- ☐ band saw, scroll saw, or saber saw
- ☐ tin snips
- ☐ bendable straightedge (or make multiple marks)

How to do it

1 Gather your materials and adjust the location and pattern of the wooden ends proportionately to the sample pattern.

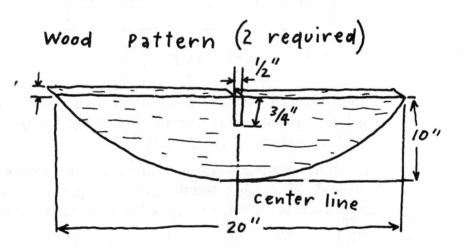

2 Make a full-size pattern from cardboard, or simply lay out the points on the wood ends and "connect the dots."

3 Using the saw of your choice from the materials list, cut out the shape, then put in the appropriate notch.

4 Next, cut the wooden web members at a length as shown. Remember, these should be short enough to accommodate the end pieces in the overall length (the sheet metal length). Predrilled pilot holes for the screws will minimize wood splitting.

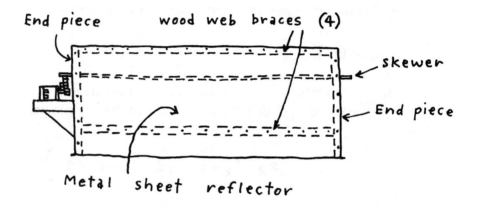

Metal sheet reflector

5 Attach the web members, which are used for strength and stability, in a manner so that the direct bottom of the parabola is clear for easy cleaning.

6 Install the motor and gearset mount at the appropriate side of the skewer notches. Test the location by placing the skewer rod loosely between the notches. Do not attach the motor and gearset yet.

7 Turn the wooden frame over, and tack the sheet metal to the underside of the frame as shown (see the illustration on the next page).

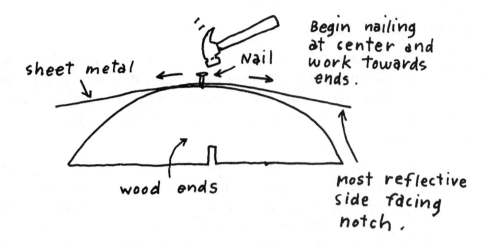

sheet metal

Nail

Begin nailing at center and work towards ends.

wood ends

most reflective side facing notch.

8 Install the motor and gearset. You must find a place for either the battery source or the photo cell, whichever method you have chosen. Wire to the motor with an on/off switch and test.

9 Line the sharp skewer rod with plump, juicy hot dogs.

10 Place the entire assembly in direct sunlight, and watch the hot dogs actually begin to glow.

11 Wait 5 to 10 minutes, and eat. Repeat steps 9 through 11 as necessary.

Cooking tips

The solar cooker always should be directed toward the sunlight. At noon, it should be focused straight up. During other hours of the day, you will have to turn the cooker toward the rising or setting sun. Get the sun while it's hot!

Project 12

Cool ideas

Obviously, there are hundreds, if not thousands, of devices and applications in which solar energy provides the power. It would be too easy to suggest that you dream up that next solar-driven device. Instead, consider these obstacles you might overcome along the way.

☐ Solar collectors have to cover a wide area in order to get usable power. Focusing the sunlight helps to raise the level of concentrated intensity. What other factors can help? Different levels of reflectivity in the sheet metal? The depth of the skewer within the parabolic shape? This project did not call for precision accuracy in locating the focus, but solar power plants go to this extent in order to get every drop of sunshine! Should the skewer's depth be higher or lower?

☐ Can you think of any other good, practical uses for concentrated light and sunshine?

☐ Are there any similarities with these principles and fiber optics? Lasers? Magnifying glasses and starting a fire?

☐ What other culinary products can you make on our solar cooker? How about one big enough for a pig roast?

☐ Could you roast the hot dog buns on a modified unit?

☐ You can see how shape can affect the wave direction. Any other shapes worth trying? How about an ellipse?

Sun dogs

We are all well aware that our natural resources and fossil fuels will be depleted someday. What will be the energy alternative? It's got to be out there! Thousands of people have tried to come up with a safe, economical, good-for-the-environment solution. One new technology is called *spheral solar*, which magnifies the surface area for a given solar collector by using millions of spherical built-up units on a collector. What can you come up with?

As humankind strives for the solution, all efforts could and should be focused toward the sun!

Glossary

alternating current (ac) An electrical current whose direction is changed 60 times per second. This is the common electricity found in most homes.

anode The negative node, or terminal, or a battery; the positive electrode of an electrolytic cell.

armature The rotating element of a dc motor. In motors, it is usually made up of an iron core wound with wire. Current is brought to this component via the commutator.

brushes These devices are necessary to a dc motor's operation. They transmit the electrical current to the commutator on a dc motor by actually touching the commutator.

cam A round or wheel-like device with an irregular shape, which provides an irregular motion as it rotates.

camshaft Used in most automobile engines, it moves all the rods within an engine's cylinders; uses several cams to maintain a specific timing within the engine.

capacitance The amount of stored energy in a capacitor.

cathode The positive node, or terminal, of a battery; the negative electrode of an electrolytic cell.

centrifugal A force that tends to act in an outward direction, away from the center or axis. Many pumps and fans are centrifugal by design.

circuit The full and complete path of an electrical current, including all the components that affect that current.

commutator The element on a dc motor that takes the electrical current from the brushes and passes it through the armature, thus allowing rotation.

conductive In electrical terms, that which allows for the flow of electricity; the opposite of *resistive*.

cubic feet per minute (cfm) The designation for the amount of volume a pump or fan can displace in one minute.

designing by replication Making anything or building a project using a pre-existing model to work from or to duplicate. When you design by replication, you can keep the same, basic design (that has proven to be a good one) and change it in your own way to make it better.

direct current (dc) An electrical current that flows in one direction continuously. This is the electricity found in most batteries.

drivetrain All the components connected between a motor shaft and the object being moved. Examples are couplings, gears, belts, chains, sprockets, and other shafts.

dynamic The principle that has to do with the action of force on objects in motion.

electrode A conductor used to make electrical contact with a nonmetallic component in a circuit. Example: the positive and negative terminals of a battery.

electrolyte Any compound that can carry electrical current and is eventually broken up into its individual parts by that current.

electromagnetic induction The principle, largely developed by Michael Faraday, in which a stronger magnetic field is created by passing a lesser magnetic component through the region of a current carrying conductor. This is the basic premise for most ac and dc motor operation.

farad Named after Michael Faraday, this unit is used to measure capacitance.

field The stationary part of a dc motor that receives a constant, electrical voltage. This allows for interaction between the armature and the field voltages to create motion by means of electromagnetic means.

fixture A device, usually created for a specific object, that is used to hold that object in place while work is being done to it. Sometimes called a "jig."

focal point The meeting place of many rays or beams of light after they have been reflected; sometimes called the *focus*.

fossil fuels Any materials extracted from the earth that are used for combustion; examples are petroleum, coal, and natural gas.

gear ratio The relationship between two or more gears that are connected to each other; usually involves the size or diameter of the gears, as well as the amount of teeth they have. A gear ratio of 2 to 1 indicates that one gear turns twice for every one revolution the other gear makes.

gear reduction Similar to (and often used interchangeably with) *gear ratio*, this practices slows down the speed of rotating objects to make more torque, or turning power, available.

head pressure Term used in pumping applications; the amount of pressure a pump has to overcome before it can start moving a fluid. Units are in feet.

henry Unit of measure for inductance named after the American physicist Joseph Henry.

horsepower Measures the amount of power in electric motors; unit equal to the force needed to lift 33,000 pounds, one in one foot minute.

impeller Component within a pump that turns, pushing or forcing fluid forward.

in parallel Wiring practice in which components in the electrical circuit are each supplied their own necessary electricity simultaneously; this approach takes more wiring than the *in-series* method.

in series Wiring practice in which components in the electrical circuit are supplied electricity first to one component and then to the next; less wiring is required than for the *in-parallel* method. In a series circuit, if the first component fails and won't conduct electricity, the next component won't get any electricity either.

intake The section of the pump that allows for the fluid to enter so that the impeller can push it forward.

leads The terminal ends of insulated electrical conductors.

mechanical energy Any pulling, pushing, or twisting force used to do work.

mechanism A set of fundamental processes and materials that work together as part of a machine.

motion control Any action that starts, stops, reverses, accelerates, or decelerates something in motion.

nonconductive Something that does not allow for the flow of electricity.

parabola Curve shape formed by intersecting a cone parallel to a sloping side.

photosynthesis Process of creating sugars and starches in chlorophyll-containing plants by means of sunlight.

photovoltaics Technology that allows electricity to be produced directly from sunlight.

power transmission Process of converting electrical energy into mechanical energy and transmitting that energy throughout a drive train and machine.

recirculating pump system Any closed-loop pumping system that moves fluid that eventually returns to the original pump's intake section for movement again; the fluid is re-cycled.

reverse engineering Means of determining how a final product was conceived, designed, and manufactured by retracing the steps in the opposite order. Example: taking something apart to see how it was put together.

solar constant Total energy radiated by the sun for a period of time.

solar energy Any of a number of means of turning sunlight into usable power. Some solar energy systems harness heat from the sun's rays; others convert the sunlight into electricity.

specifications Description of the work to be done and the materials to be used for manufacturing a product or building something, typically lengthy and in written form.

speed Rate of motion, fast or slow; sometimes called *velocity*.

spheral solar Newer form of photovoltaics whereby miniature, spherical solar cells are produced onto sheets, greatly increasing the surface area for solar energy collection.

static An object at rest; motionless.

torque A twisting, turning force equal to a force applied about an axis; it is the force prevalent in most machines.

volt Unit that measures the force (voltage) of an electric current; named after Italian physicist Alessandro Volta.

volt-ohmmeter Electric measuring device that can detect levels of voltage, current, and resistance in an electrical circuit; typically battery-powered.

Suppliers

Here you'll find places to locate all the parts (and technical support in many cases) you'll need to complete the projects in this book. Of course, the emphasis of this book is to be resourceful. Check within your own home first. Look inside of discarded toys and appliances—always use free or cheap stuff first.

In addition to the sources listed here, check your local hardware store, or scientific and technology stores in your area. Just take a look in the phone book.

AMERICAN SCIENCE AND SURPLUS
3605 Howard Street
Skokie, IL 60076
(708) 982-0870
(800) 934-0722 (fax)
Lots of neat stuff for the hobbyist; not too expensive.

DIGI-KEY CORPORATION
701 Brooks Avenue South
Thief River Falls, MN 56701-0677
(800) 344-4539
Electronic stuff from 3M, Panasonic, AMP, etc.

EDMUND SCIENTIFIC COMPANY
101 Gloucester Pike
Barrington, NJ 08007-1380
(609) 547-8880
Should have everything you will need; good technical support.

JDR MICRODEVICES
1224 S. Bascom Avenue
San Jose, CA 95128
(800) 538-5000
Electronic parts catalog supplier; good prices and service

NEWARK ELECTRONICS
4801 N. Ravenswood Avenue
Chicago, IL 60640-4496
(312) 784-5100
Electronics distributor; call or write for catalog and local office.

RADIO SHACK
A Division of Tandy Corporation
P.O. Box 2625
Fort Worth, TX 76113
(800) THE SHACK
They have answers to your electrical questions—and most of the hardware, too!

W.W. GRAINGER CORPORATION
5959 West Howard Street
Chicago, IL 60648
(312) 647-8900 or (800) CALL WWG
Great source for tools, motors, power transmissions, and electrical supplies; hundreds of branch locations across the U.S.

...And, if by chance you need to get a patent for your invention, you'll find this address helpful:

UNITED STATES PATENT AND TRADEMARK OFFICES
Washington, DC 20231

Index

About the author

Robert Carrow lives in Harmony, Pennsylvania. He travels extensively, providing motion and control solutions for industrial applications and machines. He is an automation engineer, the father of two future inventors, and the author of several papers and books.

Win $500 CASH!

Learning Triangle Press

SciTech Sweepstakes
Official Entry Form

Name _____ Age _____

Address _____

_____

City _____ State _____ Zip _____

Country _____

Telephone ( ) _____

Parent or guardian must sign Signature Line:

Parent or guardian's name _____

Signature _____

Attach additional sheets if necessary to answer the following questions.

Contest Rules

To Enter: You may enter at any time and you may submit multiple entries. You must use the entry form in this book, which may be photocopied. Fill out the form completely and submit it with a nonreturnable photograph of your project. If you are one of the five finalists selected by the panel of judges, you will be contacted to submit your project. Failure to submit your project if you are a finalist will result in disqualification.

Eligibility: Anyone ten through sixteen years of age may enter, excluding employees of McGraw-Hill and their dependents. A parent or guardian over the age of 21 must sign on the Signature Line.

How a Winner Is Selected: A panel of judges, each of whom is active in the field of industrial technology, is selected by Learning Triangle Press, an imprint of McGraw-Hill, or its representatives. This panel determines the five finalists and the winner. The judges' decision will be based on practicality, creativity, and originality and will be final.

Prizes: A prize of U.S. $500 will be awarded annually. All entries received from June 1 of one year through May 31 of the following year compete for the same award.

Winner's List: For the name of the winner in any year, send a self-addressed, stamped envelope, between August 15 and December 15 of the year in question, to SciTech Sweepstakes, Learning Triangle Press, Associate Director of Marketing, 11 West 19th Street, New York, NY 10011.

All federal, state, and/or local rules and regulations apply. Void where prohibited by law. Winners are responsible for any and all taxes associated with their acceptance of any prize. Sponsor is not responsible for misdirected or illegible entries. In the event that any winners fail to accept their prizes or fail to meet the eligibility requirements, the unawarded prizes will be awarded to a runner-up contestant. Winner will be required to sign a release and affadavit that, among other things, will permit use of winner's name and a description of the winning entry in publicity materials.

Describe your invention.

_____

_____

_____

_____

_____

_____

_____

What pages of the book were most helpful?

_____

_____

Which projects from the book did you build?

_____

_____

What did you learn?

_____

_____

_____